LIVE UNOFFENDABLE

Patricia King Ministries
PO Box 1017
Maricopa, AZ 85139

LIVE
UN
OFFENDABLE

PATRICIA KING
Foreword by James W. Goll

ENDORSEMENTS

CHÉ AHN

"In these polarizing times, one of the biggest challenges—for believers and unbelievers alike—is to overcome offense. My dear friend Patricia King writes from the heart as she shows us a better way to live, overflowing with God's love instead of offense. No matter your background, culture, or calling, this book has something to offer you. *Live Unoffendable* is a must-read for this generation."

DR. CHÉ AHN
SENIOR PASTOR, HARVEST ROCK CHURCH, PASADENA, CA
PRESIDENT, HARVEST INTERNATIONAL MINISTRY
INTERNATIONAL CHANCELLOR, WAGNER UNIVERSITY

CINDY JACOBS

"Every believer needs to read this book! As I did, the Holy Spirit challenged me and showed me there were situations I needed to deal with. I am definitely a better Christian and closer to God for applying its truths."

CINDY JACOBS
GENERALS INTERNATIONAL

ELIZABETH TIAM-FOOK

"From the first chapter to the last word, Patricia King has brilliantly invited each reader to embrace the Cross in a deeper way and to *Live Unoffended*. I have watched her humility in situations where she could have been offended but chose to think the best of others, walked in love, and even served those that hurt her.

"This book will challenge you. This book will inspire you. This book will invite you into a Kingdom journey of love and to truly walk and live an unoffendable life."

ELIZABETH TIAM-FOOK
INTERNATIONAL YOUNG PROPHETS, FOUNDER
MARICOPA, ARIZONA

STACEY CAMPBELL

"Because of her life-long pursuit of being unoffendable, Patricia King speaks from her heart and not just her head (Matthew 7:29). One will not be able to read very far into this book without recognizing how easy it is to become offended and how difficult it is to overcome the sin of offense. We all need the truths espoused herein. Written with grace and truth, this book has the power to change culture—first in the individual, then the home, the church and, ultimately, society. This is a book for everyone, and I highly recommend it."

STACEY CAMPBELL
SHILOH GLOBAL
WESLEYSTACEYCAMPBELL.COM

JOAN HUNTER

"Patricia King's book, *Live Unoffendable,* is a timely, powerful and insightful dose of divine medication for today's tidal wave of shallow, self-centered Christianity. This book needs to be widely disseminated among believers throughout the world. God's people do perish for a lack of knowledge about this very subject. That is why I am so excited that Patricia King has released this work. Now read it and put it into practice because this is an essential element of Christian life. A great word to all of those in the church."

JOAN HUNTER
AUTHOR/HEALING EVANGELIST
HOST OF MIRACLES HAPPEN! TV SHOW
WWW.JOANHUNTER.ORG

BARBARA J. YODER

"We are living in an era of division and offense. Almost everyone is on edge, ready to fight one another to the bitter end. This should not be so in the body of Christ. We can be right but terribly wrong. Patricia King lays out a clear path for how to think about offense and how to respond from a godly, biblical standpoint. If we are going to impact the world the way we are admonished to biblically, we must grow up and learn how to deal with division, differences, and offenses. We desperately need this book by Patricia. Love is the bottom line. Love does not take offense."

BARBARA J. YODER
FOUNDING AND OVERSEEING APOSTLE
SHEKINAH CHRISTIAN CHURCH
WWW.SHEKINAHCHURCH.ORG

MICHELLE BURKETT

"Jesus said that the world will know us by our love… Yet, sadly, too often what the world sees is a church clouded by offense. In *Live Unoffendable*, Patricia King makes clear how damaging offense is, and it's scary! The tendrils of offense infect every aspect of our lives, constricting us in spirit, soul, and body. Most importantly, it dims our love. To live and flow in lavish and pure love, shining for the world to see, our hearts MUST be clear from the pollution of offense. This is a book everyone needs to read—I know I did. Let the clouds of offense part. Let us be powerfully unoffendable!"

MICHELLE BURKETT
DIRECTOR OF PATRICIA KING'S WOMEN IN MINISTRY NETWORK (WIMN)
MICHELLE BURKETT MINISTRIES

ANA WERNER

"If I speak in the tongues of men or of angels, but do not have love, I am only a resounding gong or a clanging cymbal" (1 Corinthians 13:1). Ouch! Paul doesn't hold back with this warning to us all. Pursue love above everything else. I have seen how allowing offense into our hearts is like opening the door to the enemy and inviting him in to set up camp in our lives. It's the #1 cause of sickness. Who better than a respected Apostle of Love, Patricia King, to write this very timely book? *Live Unoffendable* is Patricia King's very core life message and will bring much freedom and healing to you!"

ANA WERNER
SEER PROPHET
FOUNDER, PRESIDENT, EAGLES NETWORK
AUTHOR THE SEER'S PATH

ROBERT HOTCHKIN

"No one has ever had more right to take offense over injustice, unrighteousness, and wickedness than Jesus. Yet, He never did. There are few things more anti-Christ and self-ish than offense. It mires us in the what-about-me fowler's snare that hardens hearts and severely limits us from being able to represent the presence, power, and personality of our God in Whose image we are made. Patricia King's new book, *Live Unoffendable*, is potent and important. It will open your eyes (and your heart) to the dangers of offense and the subtle ways we often give place to it. It will also help you see the traps and limitations of offense. Thank you, Patricia, for writing this book! It may well be the missing ingredient needed to propel us into the sustained move of God that we and all of heaven have been crying out for."

ROBERT HOTCHKIN
FOUNDER, ROBERT HOTCHKIN MINISTRIES / MEN ON THE FRONTLINES
ROBERTHOTCHKIN.COM

JIM AND BECKY HENNESY

"Patricia's personal 'Love War' results in a pointed and powerfully redemptive message—strategic and timely—as the Body of Christ enters her greater glory. Patricia's heart for unity roars hope and healing through the pages of *Live Unoffendable*. The Hennesys are personal beneficiaries of Patrica's loving wisdom and we believe her Spirit-inspired words carry the capacity to truly advance the spirit of revival and unity among God's beloved."

PASTORS JIM AND BECKY HENNESY
TRINITY CHURCH, CEDAR HILL, TEXAS

PATRICIA ROSELLE

"This book is a must-read for every person because we all get offended. In this book, Patricia provides powerful, God-given insight and practical instruction on how to live an unoffendable lifestyle. I would encourage this brilliant book to be a yearly read."

PATRICIA ROSELLE
CO-FOUNDER , KING OF KINGS WORSHIP CENTER, BASKING RIDGE NJ

JOSHUA MILLS

"I am so glad that my friend Patricia King has finally written this book! It is a gem. I remember walking with Patricia during the season of her love-test, or 'Love War,' as she likes to call it. Watching the way she gracefully handled difficult situations and delicately positioned herself toward loving God and loving others (including her enemies) through it all—with an unoffendable spirit—set an amazing example for us to follow in life and ministry. I have learned so many valuable lessons from Patricia, and you will too, as you glean from the pages of *Live Unoffendable*. We cannot afford to be offended in this hour... too much is at stake! This message is needed now, more than ever before, in the body of Christ. Read it, receive the freedom God offers... and walk in the light of His glory!"

JOSHUA MILLS
BESTSELLING AUTHOR, MOVING IN GLORY REALMS
INTERNATIONAL GLORY MINISTRIES
WWW.JOSHUAMILLS.COM

MATT SORGER

"The number one strategy the enemy uses against us is to get our hearts offended. He knows if we allow offense to get into our hearts, it can short-circuit the blessing God has for us. Patricia King not only reveals the consequences of offense but shows you the way out so nothing stops the flow of God's goodness in your life. I love Patricia's message on this topic. It carries so much weight because of the purity of her heart and the love walk she models for all those around her. She has lived this message. *Live Unoffendable* will release an impartation of love, forgiveness, and power into your life."

MATT SORGER
FOUNDER OF MATT SORGER MINISTRIES AND RESCUE1, PROPHETIC MINISTER
AND AUTHOR OF GOD'S UNSTOPPABLE BREAKTHROUGH
MATTSORGER.COM

BEN AND JODIE HUGHES

"Many ask how to prepare for the days that are upon us. *Live Unoffendable,* by our dear friend Patricia King, is a practical prophetic blueprint that, once applied, will disable one of the enemy's greatest weapons against the body right now. You'll be fortified to not just withstand the temptation of offense, but to rise up in new authority, smashing strongholds that limit you.

"Live Unoffendable isn't just a book, though—it's a blazing word of fire dropped directly from heaven for this hour. Its words are charged with power to equip you to prevail!

"We not only highly recommend this book, we unequivocally recommend its author to you. Patricia King lives this message every day like nobody else we know. Her walk with Jesus challenges us constantly to love and live "better," and these pages will do the same for you!

Patricia King is a true General in the army of God, and *Live Unoffendable* is your divine battle order that will guard your heart and serve to prevent you from missing the fullness of this season.

Read it, apply it, and be the devil's worst nightmare… unoffendable and ready for battle!"

BEN & JODIE HUGHES
POUR IT OUT MINISTRIES
WWW.POURITOUT.ORG
REVIVALISTS, AUTHORS, TV HOSTS

BENJAMIN DEITRICH

"In an age of cancel culture, our modern society seems to thrive off of offense. The bigger the offense and the more drama surrounding it, the better it seems to "sell" as it attracts a crowd of people waiting eagerly for every juicy detail. This culture has not only affected the world but also the church. The rate of turnover in churches seems off the charts as people accuse and find fault with leaders, hop from church to church, and never really seem to settle anywhere. Offense is a trap, and so many of us seem to be snared in its deadly jaws.

"But there is a solution to this bondage and you hold in your hands an incredible resource toward gaining victory. In her book, *Live Unoffendable*, Patricia King outlines a path to breaking the teeth of the snare of offense. Her insights will cause God's people to live a life of abundant love, free of the resentment and bitterness offense can bring. As you journey through each page, fresh life will be imparted to your soul as well as profound truth that will set you free. Enjoy!"

BENJAMIN DEITRICK
FOUNDER, IGNITE MINISTRIES INTERNATIONAL

KIM AND PAUL OWENS

"A very much needed word for a fruitful Christian life! Patricia has masterfully compiled and delivered great revelation on the topic of forgiveness and living without offense. You will be challenged and changed."

PAUL & KIM OWENS
FRESH START CHURCH
PEORIA, AZ

TABLE OF CONTENTS

FOREWORD

James W. Goll

O ver the years, I have had the distinct privilege of observing the life and ministry of Patricia King. I have observed as she has taken up her cross, died to self, and lived unto Christ. I have seen how she has chosen, like few others, to wage a 'Love War,' forgive, and fight for the sake of others. She doesn't care if she wins the argument, she wants the cause of Christ to move forward and for Jesus to win the rewards of His sufferings.

Patricia is known around the globe for her pioneering spirit in prophetic evangelism, expansive media, pioneering work in the e-church, making a way for other women in ministry and leadership to emerge, the joining of the generations and so much more! She is always sharing her platform with some new emerging leader in some part of the world. I love that about Patricia King. All of us love that about this forerunner in Christ Jesus.

AN ENCOUNTER WITH CONVICTION

Over the last twenty years of our partnership in ministry, I have heard Patricia share on a wide range of subjects. In April of 2022, at the Harvest International Ministries annual leadership summit in Pasadena, CA, I heard her share a portion of this message. When this message was over, I turned to her and stated that I believed it was the singular most convicting message I had ever heard her give. Her personal assistant overheard my remark, and she assured me that this was just the tip of the iceberg and that there was a lot more that Patricia had under her belt to unpack on Living Unoffendable. I knew that statement had to be true. As previously stated, I have observed her live this message.

Over the years, I have observed that there can be a marked difference between ministering out of revelation and living out of a place of consecration. When a person has incarnated their revelation, there is an impartation that can occur. They have become an embodiment of that word—the word has become flesh. It is incarnational Christianity. Conviction then follows the preaching of that truth—it is not merely a theory—it is a living reality.

I have chewed on reasons why Patricia's message hit me so hard that day as the aftereffects have stayed with me. Maybe it was because I needed to hear that piercing truth, "You can live an offendable life." I remember saying, "Amen!" as I sat in the front row of Ambassador Auditorium that day and sighing, "Oh me!" I knew that sense. I knew that feeling. Truth was entering me. The light of God's Word and Spirit was penetrating my soul and exposing a thorny issue of pain, hurt, disappointment, and something called offense. In James Goll? Not me! Why, I forgive daily. Or so I thought…

Bob Jones, the late seer-prophet, taught us that forgiveness is like a yo-yo. You throw it out and it just seems to come back. You did forgive, but for some reason, it just rolls back at you. You throw it out again. Guess what? It comes back. *Now, how many times do we need to do this forgiveness stuff? Seven times, is it?* So we try to get rid of it one more time, and we toss that yo-yo out one more time, and here it comes rolling back right at us! Bob used to chuckle and then say something like, "Then there comes a day you toss that yo-yo out one more time, and the string breaks, and it never comes back again. The hold of unforgiveness has been broken. Your forgiveness is now complete."

LOVING THE SERMON ON THE MOUNT

I have always loved the teachings of Jesus and His brilliant Sermon on the Mount—but some things are easier taught than lived. Years ago, I was given a vivid dream where one of God's chosen vessels came to me and stated, "*You are never too old for the Sermon on the Mount!*" Did you know that? Some lessons we take over and over and over again. You might pass them in one season and then you face them again in another season.

Thank God for the great grace of God! And thank God that we do get to retake certain lessons in life over and over again. He wants us to become transformed and become more like His Son than we even want to!

In your hands, you hold keys to how to get rid of toxic waste in your life. You do not want to be a spreader of unhealthy toxic waste – not in the day in which we live. It's true – you can rise above the worldly system and the worldly ways, and you can live as Jesus lived. Why? Greater is He who is in you than he who is in the world. The Unoffendable One lives inside of you.

Draw on Him. Call upon your inner warrior. All things are possible! You can *Live Unoffendable* by the grace of God and leave a sweet fragrance of Christ. Yes, you can be more than a conqueror!

LOVING CHRIST AND HIS WAYS!

JAMES W. GOLL

GOD ENCOUNTERS MINISTRIES

INTRODUCTION

Patricia and I spoke and smiled often prior to the publication of this book. We agree that it is much easier to teach biblical principles than it is to translate them into our daily behavior. Oh, the irony of going to lunch with other Christians after a high-impact worship service, only to be offended by someone in the parking lot... at church... or other drivers... or the server who brought us the wrong order... or any number of other "slights" in the enemy's massive warehouse of stumbling blocks!

Harboring offenses will always hamper our efforts to be "transformed into [the image of Christ] with ever-increasing glory" (2 Corinthians 3:18 NIV).

In 1846, the poet Longfellow, a follower of Christ, wrote, "Though the mills of God grind slowly, yet they grind exceeding small; though with patience He stands waiting, with exactness grinds He all." On your journey to "unoffendable," God will bring you through seasons of grinding. If you are offended by this (sorry), take comfort in a lesson King David learned while tending his father's sheep.

Before engaging Goliath in battle (1 Samuel 17:40), David went to a stream in the desert and chose five smooth stones. Why? Rocks in the desert have sharp, hardened edges; but when rocks are submerged into the motion of the stream, hard edges grind face-to-face, beginning the painful, but beautifying, smoothing process. David knew that only stream-stones would fly straight into the forehead of Goliath.

We are those stones in God's sling. Jump into Holy Spirit's "streams in the desert" (Isaiah 43:19), and let the grinding process begin! Wave goodbye to poisonous offenses! Jesus was manifest to "destroy the works of the enemy" (1 John 3:8). He said, "As the father has sent me, so I send you" (John 20:21).

It is time to take down some giants!

PETER ROSELLE
CO-FOUNDER, KING OF KINGS WORSHIP CENTER,
BASKING RIDGE, NJ

CHAPTER ONE

"Love does not traffic in shame and disrespect, nor selfishly seek its own honor. Love is not easily irritated or quick to take offense."

—*1 Corinthians 13:5 (TPT)*

OFFENDABLE? NOT ME!

CALLED TO WAR

During a season of intense public persecution and assault for my beliefs in the supernatural, the Lord called me to a "Love War." This call to war demanded that I position my heart in love toward all who were treating me unfairly. I was called to use love as a powerful weapon amid the battle. That season worked in me a deep, lifetime commitment to love. Learning to love became my primary pursuit in life.

1 Corinthians 14:1 teaches us to make love our greatest aim, and 1 Corinthians 13:1-3 further reveals that if we do not have love, we have nothing, we are nothing, and we profit nothing. In other words, we can minister with a great anointing, be known for outstanding benevolent acts, operate in mountain-moving faith, and be successful and fruitful in our careers and earthly pursuits, but if we don't have love, it is all in vain and void of eternal value. Love is the key. Love is the foundation that we are to

build life on, for God is love. If we are building our life on God, we are building it on love.

In my love journey, I used the attributes of love that Paul disclosed in 1 Corinthians 13:4-7 as my plumbline. Love is:

Patient

Kind

Not jealous

Not proud or arrogant

Does not act rudely

Not selfish or self-seeking

Not provoked or offended

Does not hold grudges

Does not keep track of wrongs

Does not rejoice in unrighteousness

Rejoices in truth

Bears all things

Believes all things

Endures all things

I wish I could testify that I have fulfilled my love pursuit, but I have NOT! In fact, the more I gaze upon Love Himself, the more I see how much I fall short. Even though I desire to be further along in my goal to mature in love, I am truly thankful for the journey and all I am learning and experiencing.

This book highlights one glorious aspect of love: love is unoffendable!

I'M NOT EASILY OFFENDED!

I never thought of myself as one who easily entertained offense. I was convinced that I was bent toward seeing the best in all people and all circumstances. When I accepted the Lord's invitation to live unoffendable as part of my love pursuit, I thought it would be fairly easy, as I was not easily offended... until I was. The Holy Spirit began to unfold what it means to live unoffendable according to His standard and not mine. I quickly began to see that I gave in to the temptation of offense more often than I was aware. I was deeply convicted and realized I was blinded to degrees of offense I had chosen unintentionally. Offenses are not given—they are taken, and I had taken a few... more than I cared to admit at the time! Some of them I had wrongly accepted as "justifiable," and others were so subtle that I hadn't considered labeling them as offense.

I'm glad I accepted this love challenge because it made me aware of how the enemy is aggressively at work to bring great destruction through offense, while most of the time we don't even realize we are walking in it. If we are to have love established in our lives, then we must embrace the goal to live without offense.

WHAT DOES THE BIBLE SAY ABOUT OFFENSE?

Let's take a look at the following scriptures and discover the instruction they give us.

1 Corinthians 13:5
"Love does not traffic in shame and disrespect, nor selfishly seek its own honor. Love is not easily irritated or quick to take **offense**." (TPT)

Proverbs 12:16

"If you shrug off an insult and refuse to take **offense**, you demonstrate discretion indeed. But the fool has a short fuse and will immediately let you know when he's **offended**." (TPT)

Proverbs 18:19

"It is easier to conquer a strong city than to win back a friend whom you've **offended**. Their walls go up, making it nearly impossible to win them back." (TPT)

Proverbs 24:19

"Don't be angrily **offended** over evildoers or be agitated by them." (TPT)

Psalm 141:5

"When one of your godly ones corrects me or one of your faithful ones rebukes me, I will accept it like an honor I cannot refuse. It will be as healing medicine that I swallow without an **offended** heart. Even if they are mistaken, I will continue to pray." (TPT)

Psalm 119:165

"There is such a great peace and well-being that comes to the lovers of your Word, and they will never be **offended**." (TPT)

At this point, you might be questioning your own heart regarding offense. Do you at times respond with offense when you face challenging people or situations? If so, in no way am I trying to condemn or shame you. I know that if you are reading this book, it is because you want to be like Jesus, who is full of love, forgiveness, and faith. I am eternally grateful that on the cross, Jesus did not harbor even a drop of offense toward us. If He had, none of us would be saved. He was, is, and always will be, unoffendable!

Jesus said that His disciples are identified by their love (John 13:35). You probably agree that we who name Christ as our Savior, unfortunately, are not generally known for our love yet, but this must be our goal. Love is the greatest power in the universe, and we will not overcome without it. When offense is in operation, then love is not. When love is in operation, offense is not.

I want to be like Jesus, and I'm sure you do too! The bar has been raised through Christ's finished work on the cross, and we are invited to accept this awesome love challenge. We are not alone in the journey. The Holy Spirit is walking with us closely, granting grace and empowerment to pursue a life that is unoffendable and filled with love. We can do all things through Christ who strengthens us.

—〰—

When offense is in operation, then love is not.

When love is in operation, offense is not.

—〰—

Bonus Message

"My Call to Live Unoffendable" (My Jesus Stories)

To watch the message, place your phone camera over the QR code and click on the link that appears.

CHAPTER TWO

"God is not mocked, for whatever a man sows, that he will also reap. For he who sows to his flesh will of the flesh reap corruption..."

—*Galatians 6:7-8 (NKJV)*

OFFENSE IS DANGEROUS

The year 2020 was a defining year as we launched into a new era. The nations were soon struck with a global pandemic that terrorized the masses with fear, death, economic uncertainties, and cruel controversies over whether individuals should wear masks, comply with social distancing regulations, or get vaccinated. In addition to these issues, the United States was jolted with violent racial tensions and nasty political upheavals during the presidential campaign and election that gained the attention of nations around the world. Offense was running rampant through the voices of politicians, news anchors, reformers, advocates, preachers, prophets, political analysts, athletes, medical practitioners, and scientists. Many average individuals were also determined to give expression to their heated offenses in the company of any individual who would listen and through mass distribution on social media.

During that season, it seemed you couldn't post anything on social media without a backlash of angry and aggressive responses. Offense had found its platform in news broadcasts, pulpits, workplaces, family dinner tables, schools, media portals, emails, texts, and you name it! Maybe you can personally relate to engaging in some of these battles fueled by offense. The poisonous substance of offense was sent by our spiritual enemy, the devil, into the nations to weaken them so he could divide and conquer. Offense was indeed a deadly and infectious spiritual virus that was conquering the souls of men, women, and children everywhere. This spiritual pandemic of offense emerged at the same time as the covid virus. Offense, however, is more lethal than any natural virus.

FEELING JUSTIFIED?

Offense can cause a person to feel justified and powerful, but bitter offense will never produce godly justice or righteous reform on any level. Offense must be treated as an enemy if we are to see God's Kingdom advance in the earth. Offense will always weaken you. Some would argue that offense is necessary in the confrontation of evil, but there are ways you can activate righteous indignation to raise the "bar of truth" high while powerfully confronting injustices in love and without engaging in offense.

Many Christians, unfortunately, ate the poison of offense as they did not discern the assault or the enemy's purpose to destroy and control through it. I have already mentioned some of the

—␉—

Offense must be treated as an enemy if we are to see God's Kingdom advance in the earth.

—␉—

obvious and blatant public offenses that broke out on a major scale in 2020 and beyond, but offense can be much more subtle. Let's look at some of the following and see if you relate to any of them.

EXAMPLES OF OFFENSE

1. I am driving down the highway in the passing lane, and the car in front of me is not even going the speed limit. As a result, I am miffed. Why isn't the driver getting out of my way? Don't they understand that they cannot be in the passing lane if they are not doing the speed limit and they need to move out of the way of those who are passing? They are doing this on purpose! I slam the horn (or not). I'm offended.

2. I am in a restaurant and the server brings me the wrong order. She apologizes and explains that she will send it back and have the chef prepare the proper meal. Everyone else at my table has their meal. I am in a hurry and they are taking their own sweet time in the kitchen. I am upset with the chef and the server for not caring for me as they should—after all, I am a paying customer...and by the time I get my meal, others at my table will be finished, and I will need to rush to eat my food. What incompetence! I'm offended.

3. In my workplace, a promotion became available. A co-worker with less experience than I have and who has worked fewer years with the company got the position. I wanted the position. I deserve the position! This is not fair! I'm offended.

4. I'm new to the church and have been faithfully attending for over six months, and no one has reached out to me. I feel rejected. I am upset with the carelessness and lack of love in the congregation and church leadership. I'm offended.

5. I am a gifted person and called by the Lord, but my pastor never makes room for me to fulfill my calling. I am a worship leader and musician but never get invited to the platform. I am a preacher but I am never given the pulpit. My pastor should be making a way for me, but he is not! He is not mature in his calling, and, as a result, he fails to acknowledge my gifts and abilities. I'm not seen. I'm passed over. I'm offended.

6. I have been standing in the checkout line at the department store for a long time. I chose the shortest line in order to get out quickly, but the woman in front of me needs a price check on her item, and the clerk is taking "forever" to find the information. I notice the cashier next to me has cleared her line quickly, so I grab my items to go through her checkout, and a woman jumps in ahead of me. Doesn't she know I was here first? Doesn't she know that I've been waiting? How rude! I'm offended.

7. Someone has been cruel to me and has hurt me to the core. I feel unfairly judged. I will move on, but I can't let it go. I'm hurt and will avoid that person like a plague. I'm offended.

8. I've heard that people have been talking negatively about me when I'm not there. I'm offended.

9. My boss didn't handle a work crisis the way he should have. It's easy to see his mistake; is he blinded to wisdom? I'm offended.

10. I was sick and no one reached out to me. They should have, but they were insensitive and uncaring. I'm offended.

11. I can't stand that political leader! I hate their policies, the way they speak, and the way they run their district. They should never have been elected to office! I'm offended.

12. I'm caring for my frail mother and have no help from the rest of the family. Why are they putting all the responsibility on me? I'm offended.

13. I am angry at the point of view someone shared on social media. I can't believe they have taken that stand. I disagree and hate their viewpoint—I will set them straight! I'm offended.

14. My spouse has not been sensitive to my needs. That is their duty. I'm always serving them, they should do the same for me. I'm offended.

15. God did not come through for me. He should have because His Word says so. He failed me. I'm offended.

OFFENSE IS DANGEROUS!

Once offense finds its way into your life, it begins to defile everything. On one occasion when I was preaching a message on being unoffendable, I implemented a simple object lesson. I took a glass of pure water (representing an undefiled, pure heart), and then poured into it a teaspoon of dirt (representing offense). For the most part, the dirt sank to the bottom, with a few particles floating around in the rest of the cup. You could still drink off the top of the glass without swallowing dirt (offense). I then added another spoonful of dirt (offense) and another and another. Before long, the entire glass of water was dirty. This is a picture of how offense affects our lives. The more offenses we take, the more our life is defiled.

Offense is often the root to a wounded soul, broken relationships, destroyed families, diminished Christian testimony, anxiety, blocked blessings, poverty, rejection, oppression, and emotional, mental, and physical illness and disorders. If offense is not the actual root, you will find it often to be a first response and reaction to the situations listed above. Offense is always dangerous and cannot be justified!

THE 5 DEADLY ELEMENTS OF OFFENSE

Offenses are not given—they are taken, and they do not come alone! When you choose to take an offense, you've also chosen the five deadly elements of sin that come along with it—and it doesn't stop there. Sin always bears consequences. So in taking offense, you have triggered a deadly chain reaction in your life.

"God is not mocked, for whatever a man sows, that he will also reap. For he who sows to his flesh will of the flesh reap corruption." —Galatians 6:7-8 (NKJV)

God's law of sowing and reaping teaches us that what we sow, we reap, and we always reap more than we sow. When you understand that with each offense, you are also sowing into five areas of sin and all of the associated consequences, you'll never want to say yes to offense again! Let's look at these five transgressions:

1. Anger

Offense is triggered by anger and contains anger. We don't always realize we are angry unless we are experiencing an emotional outburst, but anger is expressed through being slightly miffed all the way through to levels of violent rage.

Often, we justify our anger if it is attached to an injustice. We call it righteous indignation, however, authentic righteous indignation will rightly divide between the sin and the sinner. The wrath of God is directed against the unrighteousness, not the person (Romans 1:18), and it will work to destroy the unrighteousness with wisdom and confidence rather than through a reaction to offense.

"A man's anger does not bring about the righteousness of God." —*James 1:20*

Many ask about the difference between unrighteous anger and righteous indignation. I believe a simple explanation is that righteous indignation addresses the sin while unrighteous anger targets the person. We cannot compromise what is right and true, but indignation that is pure is directed against the action and produces righteousness.

Paul explains it well in the following passage:

Ephesians 4:25-26

"BE ANGRY [at sin—at immorality, at injustice, at ungodly behavior], YET DO NOT SIN; do not let your anger [cause you shame, nor allow it to] last until the sun goes down. And do not give the devil an opportunity [to lead you into sin by holding a grudge, or nurturing anger, or harboring resentment, or cultivating bitterness]." (AMP)

When you sow anger through your offense, it begins to work inside you. It affects your mood. It hinders you from loving well, and it separates you from the Savior's heart. This is quite a consequence in itself, but people who do not deal with their anger frequently end up having anger controlling them. As a result, they can become very destructive and abusive to themselves and others.

We are not alone in our vulnerability to offense-triggering anger. Esteemed Bible characters also struggled. For example, when Jesus was arrested after His prayer time in Gethsemane, Peter, being angry and offended, took out his sword and cut off the ear of a soldier. His heart was to defend Jesus, but Jesus had a greater mission and taught Peter an important lesson.

John 18:10-11

"Then Simon Peter, having a sword, drew it and struck the high priest's slave, and cut off his right ear; and the slave's name was Malchus. So Jesus said to Peter, 'Put the sword

---

Anger hinders you from loving well,
and it separates you from the Savior's heart.

---

into the sheath; the cup which the Father has given Me, shall I not drink it?'"

James and John were offended because the Samaritans did not receive Jesus as He was headed to Jerusalem. As a result, they were angry and indignant. They were ready to call down fire to consume them, but Jesus rebuked them and explained that His heart was to save and not destroy.

Luke 9:54-56

"When His disciples James and John saw *this*, they said, 'Lord, do You want us to command fire to come down from heaven and consume them?' But He turned and rebuked them, and said, 'You do not know what kind of spirit you are of; for the Son of Man did not come to destroy men's lives, but to save them.' And they went on to another village." (NASB1995)

Some believe that anger is not an issue to be concerned about unless it manifests in lawless or harmful behavior, but Jesus said that anger is on par with murder.

Matthew 5:21-22

"You have heard that the ancients were told, 'You SHALL NOT MURDER,' and 'Whoever commits murder shall be answerable to the court.' But I say to you that everyone who is angry with his brother shall be answerable to the court."

Angry words and actions have caused great pain and devastation in individuals and families. Anger is an element found in offense. It is a deadly transgression with many damaging consequences to both the individual operating in it and those who are the recipients of the manifestations of the anger.

2. Bitterness

One indicator of offense is how you feel when you think of someone—is your feeling bitter or sweet? For example, if I think about a person, I usually recognize a peaceful, positive, and pleasant feeling—sweet. However, if I am holding offense, the feeling is very different—a bitter, negative, or unsettled feeling in contrast to sweet. If I don't feel sweet, positive, or pleasant toward someone when I think of them, then I have to ask the question, "What do I feel?" In some cases, we might say, "I feel nothing," and claim we are emotionally neutral with no feelings. Usually, however, we are not neutral. Any negative feeling, even if it's subtle, usually has its root in bitterness and when that is the case, you can surely find offense lurking in the shadows.

The spectrum of bitterness can include light and subtle feelings of irritation all the way through to intense, bitter anguish and hatred. But, one thing is for sure; whatever the level, bitterness will begin to destroy you internally if it is not dealt with. It will rob you of peace, joy, and love.

Bitterness will make your life miserable! It can even influence your physical health. Some medical scientists have discovered that bitterness can be a contributing cause of many diseases and infirmities, including cancer, arthritis, autoimmune disorders, and heart disease.

Bitterness will also spread like a virus to others. We seldom keep offense to ourselves because, as Jesus taught, "Out of the abundance of the heart, [the] mouth speaks" (Luke 6:45 NKJV). If bitter offense is in the heart, it will be expressed through the mouth and fill the minds and hearts of those who hear. The offense is inevitably shared with others, "defiling many." You might say, "This is just between you and me; don't tell anyone else," but I think we all know that doesn't work. It spreads and then leads to bitter actions—not only thinking or speaking your offense, but acting on it.

Hebrews 12:14-15

"Pursue peace with all people, and holiness, without which no one will see the Lord: looking carefully lest anyone fall short of the grace of God; lest any root of bitterness springing up cause trouble, and by this many become defiled." (NKJV)

This passage confirms that a root of bitterness can spring up and cause trouble, defiling many. Bitterness spreads. Offense spreads.

Every one of us has at some time received someone's bitter opinion or evaluation on something, and equally, we have spread our bitter offense to others through what we communicate.

It is important to be a good listener and have a heart to help those who are struggling with difficult situations in their lives, but if someone comes to you with an offense against another, don't partner with it. Always remember that there are at least two sides to a conflict, and each side is seeing through their own lens and perspective. It is vital that you hear every side of an argument or crisis so you can help those involved walk in the character and wisdom of God as they resolve the conflict. The moment you agree with someone's offense, you lose your power to help, and their bitterness then enters and defiles you. Somewhere along the journey, you will share the passed-on offense and spread it some more. That is a dynamic you do not want to create.

Parents spread bitter offense to their children, husbands to wives, wives to husbands, bosses to their employees, friends to friends, pastors to their congregations, government leaders to those they represent, and the list goes on… and on… and on.

When you choose offense, bitterness defiles you and many others. Stay away from it at all costs. The more we are offended, the more bitterness will fill the atmosphere of our world. It never abides alone in your heart—it spreads. And when mass media and social media distribution become conduits for it, bitter offense can literally fill nations of people in a very short period. A little bitterness is like leaven that is added to a bowl of dough. The whole bowl of dough will be influenced by the leaven's power.

Let me highly exhort you at this point to avoid bitter offense at any cost and to NOT come into agreement or share another's offense.

3. Judgment

The judgment found in offense is sometimes hard to detect because it can be considered what we would call, "Just a casual opinion." I have often heard people say, "Well this is just an opinion…" and then proceed to share a judgmental and critical accusation against someone.

A woman was once offended at the way her child's teacher was instructing the class. She was sharing with a friend over coffee that she didn't think the teacher was competent and should be fired, and then added, "But that's just my opinion." That was not just her opinion; it was her offense. It was her judgment.

I have also noticed that some will label their judgment as "discernment" when, in fact, it is most often offense with a spiritual label. People will sometimes approach me with a warning about someone they are concerned about. They make a point of telling me that they have an accurate gift of discernment. They then continue to inform me that the person of concern is full of spirits of Jezebel and witchcraft, or some other sort of evil, and that I should stay away from them. But true discernment has a redemptive thread to it. It doesn't carry judgment.

Discernment can be used to warn you of impending danger so you can offer a solution such as confrontation, prayer for protection, or a specific action, but such action must not be taken due to offense or critical judgment. We act in confident, restful faith because of clear direction and wisdom given by the Holy Spirit. This holy wisdom from above is "first pure, then peaceable, gentle, easy to be intreated, full of mercy and good fruits, without partiality and without hypocrisy" (James 3:17 KJV).

True discernment has a redemptive thread to it.
It doesn't carry judgment.

God's true discernment is a precious gift and invites us to seek the Lord for His redemptive purposes, wisdom, and solutions but should never be used as a tool to vindicate offense or accusation.

Religious Judgment

Offense can also produce religious judgment demanding that someone "pays their dues." Let's confirm this with the Bible's account of the woman who was caught in adultery in John 8:3-11.

> The scribes and the Pharisees brought a woman caught in adultery, and having set her in the center of the court, they said to Him, "Teacher, this woman has been caught in adultery, in the very act. Now in the Law Moses commanded us to stone such women; what then do You say?" They were saying this, testing Him, so that they might have grounds for accusing Him. But Jesus stooped down and with His finger wrote on the ground. But when they persisted in asking Him, He straightened up, and said to them, "He who is without sin among you, let him *be the* first to throw a stone at her." Again He stooped down and wrote on the ground. When they heard it, they *began* to go out one by one, beginning with the older ones, and He was left alone, and the woman, where she was, in the center *of the court.* Straightening up, Jesus said to her, "Woman, where are they? Did no one condemn you?" She said, "No one, Lord." And Jesus said, "I do not condemn you, either. Go. From now on sin no more." (NASB1995)

These scribes and Pharisees were offended with Jesus' teachings and they tried to trap Him so they could condemn Him and

His doctrine before the people. They were also offended with the woman caught in the act of adultery. Targeted self-righteous, religious judgments can sometimes trigger offense in the best of us—but not in Jesus! When they confronted Him, He remained calm and peaceful but also very committed to the truth. He stooped to the ground and wrote something in the dirt. We do not know what or why, but He soon looked up and brilliantly raised the standard of truth in the presence of the confronters. He supported the law by not denying it, and then said, "He who is without sin can cast the first stone." This statement says a lot! Without condemning or accusing them, He revealed their own sin issues. They were all holding their stones in hand but dropped them and left for home when they realized that they too had sin.

Perhaps you or I would have been offended with the religious leaders who were accusative, but Jesus showed no offense. He then turned to the woman and asked her if there was anyone left to accuse her. She answered, "No one." The Lord responded, "I do not condemn you, either. Go. From now on sin no more."

He upheld truth but without judgment. He was the only one who could have judged her by stoning because He had no sin—but He didn't. He was not offended but was clear in His communication with her that she was not to continue to sin. He did not

Offense makes me think I have the right to hold the stone.

judge the religious leaders for their sin and self-righteousness, nor did He judge the woman caught in the act of adultery, but He did speak the truth in love.

We so often attempt to vindicate our offense by clothing it in self-righteousness. This is what the religious men in the above portion of scripture were doing. They quoted the scriptures. They knew the scriptures, and in the name of "keeping the law," they were offended. I wonder if they cared about the woman receiving salvation and deliverance or if they were only interested in seeing that "justice" would be served. Jesus said that He did not come to judge but to save (John 12:47).

There is a great exhortation for us in the following scripture that confirms the point Jesus was making with the religious leaders and the woman caught in adultery. Let's not get caught in the same trap.

Romans 2:1-4

"Well," you may be saying, "what terrible people you have been talking about!" But wait a minute! You are just as bad. When you say they are wicked and should be punished, you are talking about yourselves, for you do these very same things... Do you think that God will judge and condemn others for doing them and overlook you when you do them, too? Don't you realize how patient He is being with you? Or don't you care? (TLB)

Accusation and condemnation are part of the profile of unrighteous judgment that is tied into offense. I want to show you something powerful in Revelation 12:10 regarding accusation:

—∿—

*We tend to hold others to a higher standard
than we hold ourselves.*

—∿—

"Then I heard a loud voice in heaven, saying, 'Now the salvation, and the power, and the kingdom of our God and the authority of His Christ have come, for the accuser of our brethren has been thrown down, he who accuses them before our God day and night.'"

Four promises come into manifestation WHEN accusation is thrown down!

1. Salvation
2. Miracle working power
3. The kingdom of God
4. Christ's authority

When we get rid of accusation and critical judgment in our lives, we will see these four promises displayed. Let us not be the individuals used by the enemy of the cross to transmit accusation and judgment.

Jesus openly taught us regarding the consequence of judgment in Matthew 7:1-2:

"Do not judge so that you will not be judged. For in the way you judge, you will be judged; and by your standard of measure, it will be measured to you."

Judgment, along with its accusation, condemnation, and criticism, is one of the deadly transgressions found in offense, and it will always come back at you in greater force and measure than it was released through you. Remember, you reap what you sow (Genesis 8:22; 2 Corinthians 9:6), and you always reap more than what you sow. What you deal to others you will receive in return, "pressed, down, shaken together, and running over" (Luke 6:38).

Let us be like Jesus and allow His mercy to triumph over judgment (James 2:13), while at the same time not compromising the truth or righteous standards. Let wisdom and truth direct and motivate us—not offense-based judgment.

4. Unforgiveness

I am always surprised at how many, who have been forgiven by God of all their own sins, tolerate unforgiveness. It must be because they don't understand the consequence of unforgiveness. I've known individuals to say during personal ministry sessions, "I cannot and will not forgive!"

Jesus teaches us through a sobering story in Matthew 18:21-35 how lethal unforgiveness is. The story begins with a king who wanted to settle accounts with his slaves. One of his slaves owed ten thousand talents (a talent was worth fifteen years of labor) and was brought before the king who demanded payment. The slave, sadly, did not have the means to repay, so the king commanded him to be sold along with his wife and children for payment. The slave fell to the ground and begged for some more time to repay. The king felt compassion for him and showed great mercy by forgiving him the full debt. The slave was released from all obligation to the debt.

After being forgiven, he went out and found a fellow slave who owed him a hundred denarii (a day's wage). He seized him and choked him, demanding that he pay him immediately. The fellow slave pleaded with him to have patience and promised to repay, but he was unwilling. As a result, he had him thrown into prison until he could pay all of it back.

The king heard what had happened and was enraged with the slave who had been fully forgiven of his massive debt, yet was unmerciful to one who owed him so much less. In response, the king had him turned over to the jailers to be tortured until he paid back all his debt (which meant he was imprisoned and tortured for life).

After sharing the story, Jesus said to His disciples, "My heavenly Father will also do the same to you, if each of you does not forgive his brother from the heart."

This should put the fear of the Lord in us. Our forgiveness was a gift that we did not earn or deserve. On the cross, Jesus forgave us ALL our sins—every single one of them. What mercy! Yet, Jesus teaches us that if we do not forgive the sins of another, we will not be forgiven! This is heavy duty! My failure to forgive literally keeps me from receiving the mercy of God. I will be left with the responsibility to personally make full payment and that, my friend, is impossible. He paid a debt I could not pay, and He paid the debt He did not owe. What a Savior!

I believe almost every Christian has prayed the Lord's prayer. We pray, "And forgive us our debts, as we forgive our debtors" (Matthew 6:12). Jesus taught us to pray for God to forgive us in the same way we forgive others.

—⁂—

My failure to forgive keeps me
from receiving the mercy of God.

—⁂—

Mark 11:25-26 further confirms this through Jesus' instruction:

> "Whenever you stand praying, forgive, if you have anything against anyone, so that your Father who is in heaven, will also forgive you your transgressions. But, if you do not forgive, neither will your Father who is in heaven forgive you your transgressions." (NASB1995)

It is dangerous to withhold forgiveness.

Offense has threads of unforgiveness attached. Wherever there is bitterness, resentment, or judgment, there is unforgiveness. Even in what might seem like a small, insignificant offense, you will find unforgiveness because offense and forgiveness cannot operate at the same time.

I was trying to find a shuttle to a hotel around midnight, due to a flight delay resulting in a layover. I was tired and was given a phone number by the gate agent to order the hotel shuttle. I called the number, only to hear a voice prompt. I chose the number that matched my need only to find that there was another voice prompt. I listened to the options and chose the number that matched my need again, only to find that there was yet another voice prompt. I again chose the number that matched my need, and a recording informed me that an operator would help me when my position came up in the queue and that the wait was approximately ten minutes. I was not happy at all with this, and if I had been on the ball, I would have noticed that offense was already brewing. I waited for over ten minutes and finally got the operator. I could barely hear her, and she had a thick accent making it difficult for me to understand. As I struggled to hear, I was cut off and had to begin the regimen all over again. I was tired, irritated, and offended with the system. When I finally got an operator the second time, she was abrupt and rude, and I was at the end of my rope. Offense was in full bloom, and after I finally got the information I needed, I was harboring judgments against her, the hotel chain, and their communication system. I finally got on the shuttle and as we were headed to the hotel, the Holy Spirit convicted me of my offense. Needless to say, I repented and received forgiveness for my own responses and also forgave those who had been rude and insensitive to me.

Often with situations like that, we just carry on with life and don't realize that we have harbored unforgiveness toward someone through our offense. That unforgiveness stays in our soul until we forgive. We need to be quick to repent and quick to forgive. Don't delay by saying, "Oh, I will repent later when I spend time with the Lord." Repent right away and receive His forgiveness.

Unforgiveness can be very subtle or very blatant. I have heard many people say, "I forgive them, but I don't trust them—trust must be earned." Although the building of trust is important after a violation of trust, I often hear a tone of self-righteousness when this is stated. Sometimes the statement simply hides the unforgiveness.

When Jesus died on the cross for our sins, He forgave our sins and gave us the free gift of salvation. He did not test us to see if He could trust us with this gift. After Peter denied Jesus, He entrusted Peter with a call to be an apostolic father and pillar of the early church. This was undeserved and unmerited, but Jesus did not require Peter to earn His trust.

Love always desires the highest good for the sake of another and often the highest good and the wisest, most loving act during restoration is to wait until trust can be proven over time. If you require trust to be rebuilt, the decision must be made from a place of peace in the heart and not from offense or unforgiveness.

God does not want you set up for abuse or maltreatment in any way. So, after you forgive, loving boundaries might need to be put in place to protect both yourself and the one(s) who harmed you. Wisdom and love will direct you.

You may want to take some time right now and repent of any unforgiveness you have harbored in your heart toward anyone at any time. Ask the Holy Spirit to bring to your mind any specific situations so that you can repent and ask the Lord to forgive you. He will. Once you repent, your slate is clean, and you can keep short accounts from that time forward.

5. Pride

Proverbs 16:18 says,

"Pride goes before destruction, and a haughty spirit before stumbling." (NASB1995)

Offense puts you in a condescending position. You may not realize it, but you naturally look down with a condescending attitude on the one you are offended with. This is pride, and pride is dangerous. It is the very thing that caused Lucifer to fall from heaven with a third of the angels. He thought he was better than God and better than his fellow angels. Through his pride, he lifted himself above others; his pride produced fatal results.

Offense always carries an element of pride. Pride can be expressed anywhere from mild condescension to blatant arrogance, but it always contains the same dangerous consequence: it is destructive and will cause you to stumble and fall!

A minister once admitted that he engaged in prideful offense at a conference where he was speaking. Just before he was to speak, the leader of the meeting invited a young woman to share a five-minute testimony. Without realizing it, she spoke for over twenty minutes instead. After she had enthusiastically shared her testimony for the first ten minutes, the minister was in his seat, offended and thinking prideful thoughts: "I would never dishonor the time allotment given to me ... she should know better, and she thinks her message is powerful, but it's not! This crowd needs to hear me because my message is anointed, but she is taking up my time!" The offense in his heart intensified as time went on. Finally, it was his turn to speak. With offense fueling him, he jumped up to the platform, and, without realizing it, he went twenty minutes over his allotted time and had to be alerted by the leader that it was time for the break. He was asked to wrap up his message quickly so that the conference participants could get to the catered meal before it got cold. During lunch, he noticed that many were gathered around the young woman, sharing how

much her testimony had touched them, but no one shared affir-
mations with him regarding the impact of his message (perhaps
they were offended because their lunch was cold).

It was all very humiliating for him, but it was the consequence of offensive pride in action. Hopefully, they both learned
their lessons to honor the time restraints and to refrain from
prideful offense.

HINDERED PRAYERS, CURSES, AND BONDAGE

Many wonder why their prayers are not answered or why
they seem to be living under a curse instead of blessing. It could
possibly be because offense (along with its five transgressions) is
being harbored in their hearts and hindering the blessings and
breakthroughs from coming into their lives. We can gain some
valuable insights by examining the following scriptures.

Psalm 66:18

"If I regard iniquity in my heart, the Lord will not hear me."
(KJV)

Let's take a careful look at this in the light of the sin of
offense. If I choose to hold offense in my heart with its five transgressions, when I pray, the Lord will not hear me. No matter how
justified we might feel in our offense, it is not worth it to have
our prayers thwarted. Imagine, after praying fervently for hours,
hearing the Lord say, "Sorry, I can't hear you—you have offense
in your heart that has muffled the sound of your prayers."

As Christians, we carry concerns for our nations, but if the
church at large is offended with the government, judicial sys-
tems, law enforcement, educators, and media leaders, then our

—∞—

---

*Imagine, after praying for hours, hearing the Lord say,
"Sorry, I can't hear you—you have offense in your heart
that has muffled the sound of your prayers."*

—∞—

prayer meetings are useless. God does not hear our prayers. Perhaps this is why we have not seen more breakthrough even though we are praying fervently and attending many large intercession rallies and convocations of prayer. Perhaps our lack of breakthrough is because we come before the Lord with offense in our hearts.

A woman asked me to pray for her husband. She was full of offense toward him. He was making some painful choices for his marriage and family, and she was hurt by it. The hurt turned into offense. You could easily detect it in her conversation. She explained to me how much she had been praying and decreeing the word over him to see change, "But," she shared in frustration, "God isn't answering my prayers!" That is because He couldn't hear her prayers. Her heart was filled with the five transgressions of offense and the Lord couldn't hear her.

Invite the Holy Spirit to search your heart before you pray. Ask Him to show you any area of offense so you can repent, receive forgiveness, and be heard.

CURSES

Deuteronomy 28:15, 23

"But it shall come about, if you do not obey the Lord your God...all these curses will come upon you and overtake you.

"The heaven which is over your head shall be bronze, and the earth which is under you iron." (NASB1995)

In the first thirteen verses of Deuteronomy 28, we are taught that if we obey the Lord and His commandments, blessings will come upon us and overtake us. One of the blessings stated is that the heavens will be open over us and all the works of our hands will be blessed. That is quite a contrast from verses 15-68 which reveal all the curses which will come upon us if we disobey, including the brassed-over heaven that will hold back the blessings of God.

The nature of sin is that it carries gross and painful consequences, while obedience brings great blessings. When we live an unoffendable life, we are positioning ourselves for blessings that come upon us and overtake us. When we choose offense, we open our lives to receive the curses that come upon us and overtake us.

It's time to choose!

Romans 6:16

"Do you not know that when you present yourselves to someone as slaves for obedience, you are slaves of the one you obey, either of sin resulting in death, or obedience resulting in righteousness." (NASB1995)

When you choose offense, you've chosen your master, because you become a slave to the one you submit to. The enemy tempts you with offense because he is full of offense and wants you to partake of his nature. Don't do it! He's a cruel taskmaster and you don't ever want to be like him or under his control!

I have met individuals who are controlled by offense and its five deadly transgressions. They live a miserable life indeed. The enemy is happy to take control when you yield to him. He'll take what you give.

Let's yield to Christ and partake in HIS nature.

"Watch over your heart with all diligence,

For from it flow the springs of life."

Proverbs 4:23

Bonus Message

"The Five Deadly Elements of Offense"

To watch the message, place your phone camera over the
QR code and click on the link that appears.

CHAPTER THREE

"For since there is jealousy and strife among you, are you not fleshly, and are you not walking like mere men?" —*I Corinthians 3:3* (NASB1995)

TARGETS OF OFFENSE

WHO AND WHAT ARE YOU OFFENDED WITH?

There are many potential targets for our offense, and many opportunities regularly invite us to take offense. As you read through the following examples, perhaps you will identify with some. If so, take note and invite the Holy Spirit to work in your heart, so that instead of allowing targets of offense to be present in your life, you will only choose targets for your love to permeate.

1. Individuals who have failed and hurt us

Have you had people in your life who have failed or hurt you? Perhaps a parent, teacher, leader, boss, sibling, spouse, child, co-worker, or friend? We have all suffered from the failures of others—that is because their human nature is imperfect. We have also been those who have failed and hurt others even when we weren't trying to. That is because our human nature is imperfect. Just as you have been hurt and failed by others, you have also hurt and failed others.

Divorce courts, for example, are full of couples who have been hurt by each other. The unresolved wounds and accompanying offenses potentially destroy the marriage, its potential, and the family.

Many children live in homes that are filled with offense. They watch their parents wound each other and retaliate with offense. As a result, the children are hurt by what they see and are subject to. Ultimately, they will also learn to be offended without restraint. It is a terrible cycle that spreads from wounded and offended individuals into every realm of society.

Churches, unfortunately, are also filled with offense, even though as Christians we have the potential to be the most unoffendable of all! We find offense among Christians because they have been hurt, ignored, rejected, or misunderstood by their leaders or fellow believers.

A congregation member who was invited to serve in his church was offended when he discovered that the pastor's policy for his leadership team included the abstinence of alcohol, recreational drugs, smoking, gambling, and coarse language. As someone who enjoyed a glass of wine with dinner, he felt upset that he was asked to abstain. The pastor tried to explain that the policy was not intended to bring a person under unfair control

—∞—

Churches, unfortunately, are also filled with offense, even though as Christians we have the potential to be the most unoffendable of all!

—∞—

but was an act of love to be a safe model for others who might struggle. He stormed out of the pastor's office in anger and then proceeded to tell many that he was deeply wounded, hurt, and offended by having his freedom removed.

He left the church, spreading offense and dishonor, and attended another local congregation where he continued to share negative reports about his previous church. The new church did not have an abstinence policy, but unfortunately, the spirit of offense went with him. In less than a year, he left that church too, offended by something else. He then started a couple of his own churches that were failed attempts. Many of his sermons and interactions with his congregation were fueled by his offense.

Years later, he continued to target offense toward the original pastor by posting angry, judgmental, and bitter comments on social media. He blamed the original pastor and the abstinence policy for many of his failures. If you feel the need to leave a church, group, or place of employment because your values or beliefs are different, do so in peace, love, and honor. Don't allow offense to grip your life. It will destroy you.

Offense will always bring you down until it is dealt with. If you have been hurt, forgive and receive healing and counseling. As an added area of comment on this point, I want to give a word of caution to those who minister healing, deliverance, and counsel. I am aware that in some situations, the counselor/minister will take up the offense of the one to whom they are ministering. As those who minister to the broken, you must remain impartial. You are only hearing one side of the story, and if you come into agreement with the offense your counselee is carrying, you will not minister to them effectively.

A friend who had received some healing ministry for a painful area of their life shared with me after their ministry session that the counselor was appalled at the person who had shown injustice to them and ranted on about how wrong the leader was who hurt them. Without realizing it, they justified and vindicated the offense their counselee was carrying toward the one who had hurt them. This does not bring healing, cleansing, or true freedom. Remain unoffendable when ministering to those who share their painful stories. It is only then that you will be able to help your counselee overcome their offense and pain.

2. Those who are not living up to our standards

Unfortunately, it is not unusual to hear of parents offended with children, employers offended with employees, teachers offended with students, and sports coaches offended with their team. In many of these situations, offenses were taken because of failure to measure up to their standards.

A married couple once struggled in their relationship because the husband had very strict standards of order in his life. His clothes were carefully hung in the closet with all the creases of his shirt sleeves aligned, and his pants hung on special hangers according to their color. His drawer in the bathroom was carefully organized with a place for everything and everything in its place. He liked the fridge to be well organized with everything in its appropriate bin.

His wife, on the other hand, was a more creative person and did not relate well to his standard of order in the closet, bathroom, or refrigerator. He developed a strong offense toward what he perceived as lack of order in her life, and she developed an offense toward what she believed were unnecessary standards. Neither of them was able to let go of their offenses, so their marriage was attacked by many issues.

Before they were married, they enjoyed each other, deeply loved each other, looked forward to sharing a beautiful future together, and even growing old together, but offense changed everything. Their offense poisoned their marriage. After several years of the offenses building, they finally received some marriage counseling, but it took a great deal of work to rid their home of the impact of the offenses. It is hard to believe that a marriage can be destroyed because a tomato was put in the wrong bin, but offense is that lethal! As an added thought, consider this: Often, what is offensive to you in another person is that which will make you a fuller and more fruitful person in life if you lean into the lessons you can learn. "Iron sharpens iron, so one man sharpens another" (Proverbs 27:17).

3. Those we fear

Offense is sometimes a defense mechanism against what or whom we fear. For example, when the homosexual agenda began to emerge aggressively, many Christians became hostile toward those who identified with this group. Rather than speaking the truth in love and raising the bar on biblical morals and values with peaceful and bold confidence, many became offended with those who promoted the agenda. The root of their response was fear. They felt overwhelmed and powerless so responded with unholy, cruel retaliation. This type of reaction is unsuccessful. It is more productive to choose actions based on wisdom, faith, truth, and love. Fear-based responses never produce godly outcomes.

Offense can offer a false sense of strength and power. Often, gang members in slum areas, for example, are formed at an early age due to offense born out of fear. In these cases, fear and terror grip the heart of the youth due to the cruel violence they observe in their home or community. Out of that fear, they determine to retaliate with offense, but before long, they are led into a life of crime and cruelty. The consequence of these activities adds to the initial injustices rather than resolving them.

Sometimes, individuals are afraid of authority and man's opinions. These individuals might operate in offense toward those in authority in an attempt to overcome the fear of man and validate themselves. These attempts are always unsuccessful.

Fear is void of faith, but faith is needed to overcome. Of course, we should not remain silent when injustice is present. There are times to self-protect, but wise choices and responses are necessary. If you are overwhelmed with fear and reacting with offense, you will not discover the wise action plan that will provide the victory in the situation. Believe in God's ability to lead and guide. Don't allow fear to pull you into offense.

4. Government leaders and parties

It is common to find offense in individuals who have strong political biases. You will find a high level of "offendability" in political campaigns amongst politicians and those who support or oppose them. Often, you will hear a candidate's political speeches filled with offense and attacks toward their competition rather than using the time to share all the great solutions they would implement if elected.

It is also normal in our day to find offended masses criticizing the government leaders who hold office and the leaders of the opposing parties. We are instructed to pray for kings and all who are in authority, so that we can live our lives in peace (1 Timothy 2:1-3).

There is no instruction in scripture that encourages us to hold offense and critical judgments against government leaders. That type of bitter, pride-filled offense tears down rather than builds up. The offense breeds disunity, dishonor, and tension, which destroys and weakens nations. Our offense will not work to conform the government to God's will, but all things are possible for the Lord, and that is why He taught us to pray and believe!

5. Denominations/Churches/Church Movement

Among Christians and Christian leaders, you will sadly hear comparisons and judgments of other denominations, churches, or church movements that are triggered by offense.

I was having a meal with a group of leaders who were offended with the "seeker-friendly" model of churches. They were offended that the seeker-friendly church leaders were not open to the move of the Holy Spirit and were making judgments about their impure motives to simply draw in more people through being more open and inviting. They discussed amongst themselves how these churches were problematic to the advancement of the Kingdom of God in the earth. Offense and critical judgment filled the conversation, and the individuals who initiated the dialogue had never even attended a seeker-friendly church model.

On another occasion, I was listening to a livestream on social media where two leaders and the host of the program were openly offended with Spirit-filled believers who were operating in the gifts of the Spirit and the supernatural activities of the Kingdom of God. They were mocking, judging, and ridiculing believers who love the fullness of the Spirit, calling them heretics and dangerous. They even created little sarcastic 5-10 second video segments of extracted quotes taken out of context. They played these on auto-repeat to mock Spirit-filled Christians and to make their point.

On yet another occasion, I sat with some believers who were labeling traditional churches as religious and dead. Some are offended with house churches, others are offended with megachurches, and still others with media churches. So much offense!

It would be more advantageous for believers to lay down offenses and judgments and focus on obeying the leading of the Spirit and loving each other well. There is nothing wrong with speaking truth or presenting a healthy challenge or confrontation; but love must be the motive, and it must not be born out of offense.

At the end of the day, we will find that every expression of God's church in the earth lacks the fullness of God by itself, but together, we can manifest His very being and glory. We all need our beliefs and spiritual journey to be purified, so let us not give over to offense when we see others blinded or struggling in certain areas.

If we are truly concerned about areas of deception we are discerning, then love will lead us to pray and lay our lives down for their freedom without offense. In this place of seeking the

—ⱳ—

If we are truly concerned about areas of deception we are discerning, then love will lead us to pray and lay our lives down for their freedom without offense.

—ⱳ—

Lord with a pure heart for the freedom of another, He can grant wisdom and sometimes actions that you can implement to help.

6. Cities, Regions, Nations

Every nation, community, and region will have areas that are more blessed, more peaceful, and more desirable than others. Cities, regions, and nations carry a reputation: some of positive report and others of ill-repute.

As we were preparing for an outreach in a city in America, someone came to me and emphatically stated, "You really don't want to go there! It is a horrible place with so much crime, murder, and danger." They encouraged me to stay away because it was such a disgusting place. As they continued to share, I came to realize that they actually lived in this city and had wanted to leave for years but lacked opportunity. I suggested that perhaps God would change the city by bringing light into the darkness. The young man laughed and said, "No way—not even God can fix it!" Obviously, they were offended with their city and could not even see potential because their offense had blinded them.

If we look at cities, regions, and nations with offense in our hearts, we will never be part of seeing them reach their full potential. A month or so later, I actually ministered in that particular city and loved it. I saw God's potential and knew it was destined to fulfill God's glorious purposes.

A number of years ago, our family lived in a city in Canada that was known for its poverty and oppression. It was rejected by most who lived in the area and was referred to by many as "the armpit" of the region—that was truly its reputation! When people discovered where I lived, they would respond with disapproval. Most were offended by the city and what it represented, and therefore they failed to see its potential.

The Lord gave me vision to see the city become a place that would glorify Him. Over a number of years, as a few faithfully interceded and acted on Holy Spirit initiatives, significant change came, and it soon became favored as a city that God blessed.

Offense-based word curses and perspective will lock a city, region, or nation into oppression and bondage, but a blessing perspective can bring transformation. We have seen this happen in nations and cities around the world. There is no room for offense.

7. Ethnic or minority groups

Offense will keep you from valuing and honoring others. It is tragic to see how offense can target an ethnos or minority group and devalue individuals and groups. Offense creates cruel words and actions that bring harm to the lives of the afflicted. Often, when offense targets an individual, they are attacked with failed opportunities, and even their safety can be compromised.

Offense, with its five transgressions, is responsible for every form of prejudice. If you remove the offense, you remove the prejudice. Frequently, these prejudices are passed on through generations—they enter the bloodline. Generations later, when you ask someone why they carry offense, they often have no situation or reason to report—just an attitude and perspective that was passed down.

In our day, racial profiling is being confronted, and it is helping many to turn away from such offenses.

There are other complicated situations on the table creating offense and prejudice, such as issues of choice in sexual or gender orientations. As we have already stated, we are to separate the person from a transgression. If you believe that a particular moral choice a person has made in the realm of sexual or gender orientation is harmful and/or unbiblical, then it is important to care about the person, and in the right timing and way, address their choice in love and truth with your uncompromised conviction. Do not create a place for offense to operate toward a person, but a loving, bold presentation of truth could possibly set an individual free from a bondage.

Everyone has value. Everyone is loved by God. Everyone is precious. But the truth will set us free!

8. Those we are jealous of

1 Corinthians 3:3

"For since there is jealousy and strife among you, are you not fleshly, and are you not walking like mere men?" (NASB1995)

Paul describes jealousy as evidence of a carnal Christian— one who is controlled by their flesh nature and not the Spirit. We see jealousy operate often in young children. When I was in grade school, I had a friend whose family was quite affluent.

I enjoyed playing with her and going to her home after class. One day, while walking home with some classmates, one of them spoke very judgmentally of my privileged friend. I listened, and when I tried to say nice things about her in response, I was met with resistance from the group. What they were saying was horrible, and it hurt my heart, bringing me to tears. Arriving home in this emotional condition, my mother asked me what was wrong. I shared the situation, and she explained to me that she thought the girls I had walked home with were jealous of my privileged friend. There was much more that my mother helped me to unpack, but it was an eye-opener on how jealousy can turn a person's heart against another.

Unfortunately, I have seen this same behavior in adults – even some who are leaders in ministry. Jealousy is deadly and is not only fueled by offense, but it spreads offense. I praise the Lord that I have seldom been tempted with jealousy, but I remember a time when I was. It felt horrible! Envy and jealousy are contrary to Christ's nature. I reached out to the Lord for help to resist the temptation. He said, "Move in the opposite spirit and lavish them with blessings, kind words, and kind intentions." I did that and overcame the assault.

You will find offense behind every temptation to feel jealousy. You can overcome this too.

9. Our life situations and status

Some individuals are offended with their status in life or with situations they face.

A woman had opportunity later in life to work toward her dream to be a medical professional and had cultivated this desire for two decades. When she was in the second year of her training, her parents were in a serious car accident. After they recovered enough to go home, she was told that her parents needed a full-time caregiver. She was the only one in the family who was single and willing to serve them in this capacity, so she abandoned her education and her dream.

She initially felt disappointment in other family members who could have helped on some level but didn't. This disappointment grew over time into a full-on offense. She became resentful due to her disrupted education and career pursuit. She also wanted to be married, but because of her circumstances in life, it appeared that this dream would never be fulfilled. These disappointments produced increased remorse and great sadness, which turned into more offense. The bitter offense took all her joy in life, and she became a very angry, critical, and judgmental person.

She was offended with family members who failed to help and support her and also with her parents who tied her down with their care needs. She felt trapped and imprisoned not only by her circumstances but by her offense.

Offense will keep us from experiencing freedom and joy. God is well able to turn our sorrow into dancing and to give us wisdom and victory in any situation we might face, but offense hinders Him from operating. Offense builds a wall around us that is hard to penetrate.

Life can offer great challenges and disappointments, but when we keep our heart free from offense, there are answers and solutions available to meet every challenge.

10. God, who we believe did not come through for us

Sometimes when individuals are not coping well with disappointment and don't understand why a taxing situation or tragedy has taken place in their life, they blame God and take up an offense against Him.

Difficulties happen to everyone, but I have known a handful of folks over the years who have had more than their share! It is very sad indeed to see people suffer, and especially if there are no answers that satisfy. God loves each one of them and is full of compassion, but He is not the author of evil and should never be the object or subject of our offense.

I have seen individuals harden their hearts toward God. Their lives are most often filled with bitterness, doubt, and unbelief; they never overcome their grief and often become depressed.

Jesus taught us that we are blessed if we resist being offended because of Him. "Blessed is he who is not offended because of Me" Matthew 11:6 (NKJV).

The temptation to blame God and hold offense against Him is very real for some, but we must remember that He is on our side, and our tragedies are never His fault. We might not have answers that satisfy yet, but He will walk us through any hardship one day at a time, no matter the circumstances. He is not the author of the pain, but He will work everything together for good as we trust in Him.

Your sacrifice of worship and trust in times like this are your greatest offerings and will yield eternal fruit.

—◊—

Life can offer great challenges and disappointments, but when we keep our heart free from offense, there are answers and solutions available to meet every challenge.

—◊—

Do you identify with any of the targets of offense mentioned in this chapter? If not, be aware because, at some point in life, you will probably face temptations to target people, circumstances, regions, or possibly even God with offense. Being tempted is not a sin, but when we take ownership of the temptation and act on it in our thoughts, words, or actions, consequences are sure to follow. In another chapter, we will look at how to overcome those temptations and walk in victory.

Bonus Message

"Offense Impacts the Generation Line"

To watch the message, place your phone camera over the QR code and click on the link that appears.

CHAPTER FOUR

"Righteousness and justice are the foundation of
Your throne; mercy and truth go before You."
                                    —*Psalm 89:14*

JUSTICE AND OFFENSE

We constantly see injustices in the world we live in, and one of the most challenging opportunities offered to us in this environment is to remain unoffendable when we desire to confront injustice. Unjust actions and behaviors need to be addressed for sure, but if we address them from a heart filled with bitter anger, judgment, and offense, we will fail to see righteous results.

LESSONS LEARNED IN BANGKOK

I remember clearly the first night I stepped foot in Thailand, years ago. I was led by the Spirit during a time of prayer to fly to Bangkok. The Lord promised to reveal some insights to me regarding sex trafficking if I went.

We arrived at our hotel around dinner. After settling in, we grabbed a quick bite at a restaurant down the street. At the table next to me, I saw a western man, who looked like he might have been in his mid-fifties, with a young Thai girl who was dressed provocatively and looked about fifteen years old. Immediately, I was stirred with internal anger and great offense. I was aware that this man had "rented" the young girl from a brothel for the night or the weekend. She was trying to smile, but I discerned the fear that was gripping her. I wanted to go to the table, "punch out his lights," grab the girl, and take her back to our room for safety. Offense boiled within me. I wanted justice for her, and I wanted it NOW!

As I pondered how I could help deliver her, the Lord revealed some details regarding the man's life. He showed me that due to what he had suffered in childhood, he had never felt loved or valued. He hoped to find some relief through hiring a girl from the brothel to lavish attention on him, give him a sense of value, and fill the void.

At that moment, I fought intense emotional confusion. I desired to protect the girl, but I also felt compassion for the man, now that I understood some of the pain he endured in his life. The Lord revealed that both were victims of the enemy's assault and that He wanted both rescued. I realized in those moments that I was not battling flesh and blood but a demonic agenda that was targeting everyone involved. If I remained in offense, I was not going to be able to offer Spirit-led and God-initiated help to either of them.

Later that night, we walked the streets for hours where I saw more tragic situations. It broke my heart. Injustice was everywhere. It was blatant! I saw women holding drugged children.

Some of the children's legs or arms had been intentionally broken in order to increase the money given to the begging women by compassionate tourists. The women holding the children were not even their real mothers but were hired by the begging- syndicate owners.

Over the next couple of days, I became acquainted with young teenage girls who were dropped off at brothels by their own parents to make money for the family back in their villages. I met young transgender men who had taken on the appearance of women through hormone treatments and surgeries— they were working as strippers and prostitutes to entertain tourists. A few of them shared openly that they were groomed from childhood by their parents to be so-called "third gender" so they could earn significant money for the family through a life of prostitution when they were old enough. They explained that third-gender prostitutes and strippers made more money than female prostitutes.

Waves of offense and a demand for justice filled me. I was deeply distressed. I wanted to go home! I felt overwhelmed, confused, angry, and helpless. I truly wanted to leave on the next flight, but at that moment the Lord spoke to me and said, "I don't want you to go home. I want to make you a solution!" He then helped me rightly divide the battle I was fighting. The battle was truly not against flesh and blood. It was a demonic plot with real demonic enemies destroying the lives of dear people that Jesus loved and had died for. He revealed that justice would not be established through offense but through love and wisdom.

—◊—

I was to war with my indignation against the sin but to
remove my anger toward the people involved.

—◊—

I was to war with my indignation against the sin but to remove my anger toward the people involved: the brothel owners, prostitutes, handlers, sex tourists, drug dealers, organ traffickers, slave owners, and abusers. They all had a story and they all needed Jesus. They needed the truth that would set them free, but the acts of sin and the demons behind them needed to be addressed with true wrath-motivated authority. God showed me that His wrath is against unrighteousness and ungodliness and that with His power and wisdom, I could effectively wage war against the evil actions I observed. If I would find peace and repent from my offense against individuals who were contributing to the problem, He could then use me to become a solution.

That was the beginning of an amazing journey. Our team and the ministries we worked with on the ground labored together relentlessly to bring the gospel to the afflicted. Teams were formed of godly police officers, attorneys, social workers, and judges who refused to compromise through bribes, re-selling rescued victims, and other means of manipulation, greed, and corruption. Our team and others met with government leaders and people of influence to change laws and to build policies to protect the innocent and the exploited. Instead of offense, we invited God to reveal His wisdom, love, and strategies that would set captives free and raise the bar of righteousness.

We met many faithful ministers serving in organizations on the ground who had laid down their lives to free those who were bound. These laborers were and are amazing! They were all most likely tempted with offense but overcame. They allowed the wrath of God to fuel them with power to initiate and establish justice for the afflicted. They stood against the transgressions rather than the transgressors.

Many violators were arrested, tried, and imprisoned, and were offered help and guidance if they chose to make the wrongs right. The confrontation, arrest, and sentence they received was an act of love and justice for them and their victims. It offered them opportunity to turn away from crime and injustice and to live the rest of their lives empowered to do good and to fight for righteousness if they chose.

Over the course of time, children have been rescued, families restored, young people have left their jobs in the bars and brothels, and of course, many have been saved, filled with the Holy Spirit, healed, and delivered. God's justice is glorious.

My heart never softened toward the sins involved in issues such as sex, organ, and drug trafficking, or slave labor, but I have grown in love for both the exploiters and the victims. I learned that offense only stands in your way of implementing true justice. God's ways are higher than ours.

THE FOUNDATION OF THE THRONE

Psalm 89:14

"Righteousness and justice are the foundation of Your throne; mercy and truth go before You." (NASB1995)

The definition of justice is:

The quality of being just, righteousness, equitableness, or moral rightness: to uphold the justice of a cause, rightfulness or lawfulness, as of a claim or title; justness of ground or reason.[1]

It is not to be confused with justice that equals punishment, retaliation, payback, judgment, or vengeance.

Godly justice puts things in right order and establishes righteousness. If you've been unjustly treated, then God wants you restored to what is right, good, and godly. He wants you healed and protected. If you see others being treated cruelly, there is a need for justice and godly alignment. God is looking for those who will effectively establish His justice and bring transformation to individuals and to society.

VIOLENT OR NON-VIOLENT JUSTICE?

I love the wisdom Solomon demonstrated when two women came before him to receive justice. They had both given birth to sons around the same time. One of the sons died and the other lived. They each claimed the living one was their own. Solomon needed to identify the true mother. In the following portion, you will see how he operated in wisdom without offense to determine the righteous outcome. You will also see how the woman who was not the true mother agreed to have the child cut in two so that if she couldn't have the son, the true mother would not have him either. You can see the offense that motivated her through selfishness and jealousy. Let's review the story.

---

1 www.dictionary.com

—∞—

Godly justice puts things in right order and establishes

righteousness.

—∞—

1 Kings 3:23-28

Then the king said, "The one says, 'This is my son who is living, and your son is the dead one'; and the other says, 'No! For your son is the dead one, and my son is the living one.'" And the king said, "Get me a sword." So they brought a sword before the king. And the king said, "Cut the living child in two, and give half to the one and half to the other." But the woman whose child *was* the living one spoke to the king, for she was deeply stirred over her son, and she said, "Pardon me, my lord! Give her the living child, and by no means kill him!" But the other *woman* was saying, "He shall be neither mine nor yours; cut *him*!" Then the king replied, "Give the first woman the living child, and by no means kill him. She is his mother." **When all Israel heard about the judgment which the king had handed down, they feared the king, because they saw that the wisdom of God was in him to administer justice.**

When you first hear the story, you are alarmed at his decision to cut the child in two. How could this be wisdom? It sounds so violent and evil, but his instruction revealed the true mother and exposed the imposter. As a result, the child and the true mother were kept safe. No violence was needed. Justice and righteousness prevailed.

CONFRONTATION IN THE TEMPLE

I have heard individuals use the biblical example of Jesus driving out the money changers and merchants in the temple as he overturned their tables to confirm that anger and violent response are justified in order to bring about justice and divine alignment. In these presentations, Jesus is often portrayed with furious indignation, being fed up with the exploitation and defilement in the temple and at the end of His rope. As a result, it is often perceived that He entered the building with a big whip in hand and in violent fury drove out the money changers and merchants. He then proceeds with great force and wrath to overturn their tables. As they leave, he yells at them, "My house is a house of prayer, but you have made it a den of thieves" (Matthew 21:13).

Although very exaggerated, it is amazing how many imagine Jesus' conduct in this way, but is that how it actually happened? Let's imagine the scene differently:

Jesus steps into the temple and goes to the tables where they are selling doves and other animals with broken legs, wings, and other imperfections. These were not acceptable sacrifices but those who traveled from afar had no other choice but to buy them as it was difficult to bring their sacrifices with them on the journey.

Jesus discerns, examines, and assesses what is happening. He then walks over to other tables where money changers are exploiting the innocent by charging excessive and unfair exchange rates. He is greatly disturbed by the injustice and realizes there is a spiritual enemy at work. He determines to rid the temple of this demonic influence and to set free those who are being treated unjustly as well as those who are caught up in the deceptive, corrupt practices. He approaches the merchants and money changers while remaining composed and at peace. He firmly commands, "You must go—you must leave the temple now!" The King James Version uses the word "cast out," but the original Greek word used is *ekballo* which has a non-violent option of use meaning:

without the notion of violence

   i. to draw out, extract, one thing inserted in another
   ii. to bring out of, to draw, or bring forth
   iii.to except, to leave out, i.e. not receive
   iv. to lead one forth or away somewhere with a force which he cannot resist[2]

As they are gathering their things, He then turns over the tables. The King James Version uses the word "overthrew," which has a connotation of violence, but the word used in the Greek is *katastrephō* which means:

to turn over or to turn under.[3]

Maybe He didn't violently kick them over. Perhaps He simply turned them over, determined to make sure the people knew they were closed for business.

He was possibly stern and full of determination but was not demonstrating angry, violent reactions. After overturning the

---

2 *Strong's Concordance*
3 *Strong's Concordance*

tables, He then spoke defining truth with peace and confidence as He boldly declared, "My Father's house is a house of prayer, but you have made it a den of thieves." This action would have caused quite a stir. Can you imagine the talk in the town? In that sense, it was a catastrophic event for the community. I am sure that many were greatly rejoicing while others were visibly offended and disgruntled. I don't believe Jesus was moved by either response. He had done what was needed to restore right order and to bring justice to the house. He continued on His journey without offense.

The New Testament introduces us to the Savior of the World. The beautiful, precious, holy Lamb of God became our sin, paid the full penalty, and then poured His righteousness into us. What a gift! What a mystery! This is not a picture of an offended God who wanted payback with violent fury, and yet, Christ's journey to the cross was indeed violent for Him. It cost Him everything! He was engaged in a violent war against sin to set us free—it was a love war that He fought with unrelenting faith and with an intensity we can't even imagine. He took no offense because of our rebellious and selfish behavior, but rather through radical, flawless, selfless love, He upheld justice and established salvation for all who would believe and partake.

There are times when aggressive and violent action is required to establish justice. Using the Civil War as an example, we know that slavery in the southern states was one of the significant issues of contention in that day. The southern confederacy was offended with the values of the abolitionists in addition to some other political differences. Due to the financial interests of the rich plantation owners who were well-invested in slavery, they took a strong stand against the North. Through their offense, they initiated an attack at 4:30 a.m. on April 12, 1861, as they fired on Fort Sumter in South Carolina's Charleston Harbor without warning.

This declaration of battle demanded defensive engagement from the North. and the Civil War began. President Abraham Lincoln was a humble man but he was also strong and fearless, ready to fight when necessary for what was right. The outcome produced justice platforms that we enjoy today. Offense and greed began the four-year war with many casualties and deaths, but the tenacity to secure justice for all won it. At the end of the war, many acts of justice were established in law.

Being unoffendable doesn't mean that you withhold from battle. Ecclesiastes 8:3b confirms that there is "… a time for war and a time for peace." We see Jesus Himself in Revelation 19:11-19 coming with an army from heaven to war against the beast and the kings of the earth who were with him. The question is, "What heart condition is initiating and fueling the battle?" It is possible to fight with great strength and determination to uphold truth and justice, yet without offense.

Being unoffendable doesn't mean that you withhold from battle.

EXAMPLES OF UNOFFENDABLE JUSTICE

The Early Church

You don't have to read too far into the Book of Acts to see injustice against believers. One of the obvious examples is that of Saul, who we find in Acts 8:3 going from house to house, dragging believers off to prison. In Acts 26:10, he testifies that he called for believers in Christ to be stoned to death for "blasphemy" and felt justified in doing so. I am sure the early church desired justice for the mistreatment, but we do not find any evidence that they were offended with Saul or engaged in any dishonor toward him. However, it is almost certain that they interceded for him because Jesus taught them to love their enemies and pray for those who persecuted them. Their prayers produced justice for them because Saul was converted and became a great apostle who spread the gospel to the nations and advanced the Kingdom for the rest of his life. Paul is still impacting powerfully today, reaching the masses with truth through his Epistles—that is unoffendable justice.

In Acts 16:16-34, we see Paul and Silas arrested, brutally beaten, shackled, and thrown into the deepest part of the prison. Why? Because they had preached the gospel to the people and cast out the spirit of divination from a girl who was enslaved to her masters. Their imprisonment was a retaliation of the enemy, but they did not show any signs of offense due to the mistreatment. Not at all. Neither did they apologize for preaching the gospel; they made it clear that they would continue to preach in order to obey God. In their prison cell at midnight, they were praying and singing praises to God. Offended people would have been grumbling and complaining but probably not praying in faith and singing. All the prisoners were listening. Suddenly, an earthquake shook the building and caused all the prison cell doors to swing wide open. All the prisoners were free.

The chief jailer was undone over it, afraid to the depth of his soul. Paul and Silas told him not to be afraid and preached the gospel to him. He and his house were saved. But that wasn't all. Paul called for the chief magistrate to come. Paul spoke the truth to him regarding the injustice of the arrest and beatings and the magistrate released them to go in peace. They stayed at the house of Lydia and strengthened and encouraged the believers with their testimony. That is justice… unoffendable justice!

Martin Luther King Jr. lived in a day when great injustices were running rampant, specifically regarding the unfair treatment of African Americans. The injustices of his day needed to be addressed. They continue to be targeted today. However, Martin Luther King Jr. opened the way for a new level of reform to begin in his generation. He addressed anger, bitter offense, and hate as he called for non-violent, yet clear confrontation of the issues. It is easy to become offended with those who are offended, but it doesn't resolve the issue.

Martin Luther King Jr. believed that "Nonviolence was the 'testing point' of the burgeoning civil rights movement. *'If we … succumb to the temptation of using violence in our struggle, unborn generations will be the recipients of a long and bitter night of—a long and desolate night of bitterness. And our only legacy to the future will be an endless reign of meaningless chaos."*[4]

---

4 TIME "Martin Luther King Jr.: His Life and Legacy," Jan. 12, 2018

MLK's dream was for the oppressors to see the error of their ways by taking a peaceful, non-violent approach. There was much to be offended over in that day if given to the flesh, but he chose to be strong in conviction and aggressive in action without bitter offense fueling the battle. To this day, King is celebrated, esteemed, and honored. There is even a national day of celebration marked on our calendars in honor of him, his example, and his work. Degrading insults, physical attacks, and cruelty are manifestations of offense. He chose the higher ground and a greater way.

Unoffendable Church Fathers

The early church was anointed with the Holy Spirit to advance the Kingdom of God—not the kingdom of man. They were commissioned by Jesus Himself to baptize nations in the Father, Son, and Spirit, and to teach them all that He had taught them. Living Kingdom life is very different from life in the natural. Those of us who are citizens of this Kingdom live by values and standards that God Himself established. Many of these values seem to be upside down to those of the world. Instead of hating enemies, we are to love them; rather than self-defending, we are to pray for those who persecute us. Rather than taking our brother to court, we are to forgive. Rather than taking, we are called to give.

The early church fathers paid a big price to preach the gospel of the Kingdom. They were persecuted by government leaders, and yet they were to keep honor when they were dishonored. Peter taught in 1 Peter 2:17 to "honor the king." In 1 Timothy 2:2, Paul teaches the church to pray for kings and those in authority. In these two passages of exhortation, the word "king" means "the leader of the people"[5] in the Greek.

In the time Peter and Paul wrote their letters, Nero was the leader of the people—a very evil one at that! He arrested, tortured, and then executed the Christians in Rome. He announced his actions publicly as many were called to watch. He made sure everyone knew the consequences they would receive for believing in Christ. He crucified some, threw some to wild animals to be devoured alive, and others were burned alive like living torches. Even though Nero was evil and was taking a strong stand against Christians and the Christ they worshiped, Peter said to "honor" the king. Paul said, "pray" for the king. The early church refused to bow to laws that forbade them to preach the gospel or force them to violate the teachings of Christ. The persecution and martyrdom they suffered as a result did not cause the early church to become ineffective. Rather, the gospel spread like an unstoppable wildfire. Was there justice for the early church? Yes—but not in the way we would think in the natural.

The early church understood "unoffendable justice." They were committed to giving to the Lamb the due reward of His suffering. That is justice. Jesus died on the cross so that every man, woman, and child could be restored to the Father and be delivered from the evil one. The early church prayed for the

---

5 *Strong's Concordance*

—m—

The early church understood "unoffendable justice."
They were committed to giving to the Lamb the due
reward of His suffering.

—m—

Lamb to receive His due reward and lived an uncompromised life of true faith.

Jesus taught His disciples to beware of the leaven of the Pharisees (religious spirit) and of Herod (political spirit)[6] so they had one focus—the preaching of the Gospel of the Kingdom. Today we have freedom in many nations to let our light shine in society's realms of influence, such as government, business, media, education, arts and entertainment, family, and religion. Many of us also have the privilege to vote for our leaders. Of course, we should honor our privilege to vote and to represent Jesus in every realm of society, but no one leader or any one of these realms in themselves can bring forth true Kingdom manifestation and justice.

We are set apart for His purposes and glory. We are in the world but not of the world. Christ taught His disciples that the world would identify them as His disciples by the love they had for each other and not by what political parties or leaders they supported. We bring reform by shining our light. The same persecution the early church encountered when they stood for the Lamb is what we will face today. May we respond as they did—may we live unoffendable.

Jesus instructs us to take up our cross daily and follow Him. God is raising up a new breed of reformers who are fueled by the desire for righteousness and justice. They are tenacious, powerful, without compromise or mixture, and filled with wisdom from above, infiltrating every realm of society. They confront evil as they speak the truth in love and are willing to respond with

6 Matthew 16:6

any action the Lord leads them to engage in, but they are unoffendable. A motivation of offense cancels the representation of Christ in any matter. The new reformers are those who contend for unoffendable justice: for the Lamb to receive the just reward of His suffering. For this purpose, we lay down our lives before Him.

Bonus Message

"Unoffendable Justice"

To watch the message, place your phone camera over the
QR code and click on the link that appears.

CHAPTER FIVE

"Therefore repent and return, so that your sins may
be wiped away, in order that times of refreshing may
come from the presence of the Lord."

—*Acts 3:19*

OVERCOMING OFFENSE

I n my journey to live unoffendable, I have discovered a few key principles that have helped me overcome. These principles will aid you in your battle against offense.

I. MAKE A QUALITY DECISION TO LIVE UNOFFENDABLE

Sometimes we receive clear Holy Spirit conviction with a call to repent and we think, "That's a great idea—yes, I really need to repent from that." We intend to act on the conviction, but if we entertain thoughts such as, "I should," or "I need to," then we probably won't. Our determined and intentional response is to be, "I will!"

Often, we fail to take our sinful choices seriously. I believe that offense is one of those sins that is tolerated by many even when there is a strong awareness of it. If you read this book and are impacted with conviction, then you must steward the conviction. Do not take the sin of offense lightly. Offense is destroying individuals, families, and nations, and it must be stopped! Its annihilation begins with you. You can fuel it or you can stop it.

I realize from my own wrestle with offense how challenging it can be to overcome, but if you make a solid commitment to live unoffendable, it will raise the standard in your own heart. When you make a quality decision, then grace is available to help you overcome.

Your victory over offense begins with being intentional. Don't procrastinate. Make a determined choice to live unoffendable.

2. REPENT FROM OFFENSE

The word "repent" in the Old Testament is in reference to making a turnaround: turning away from evil and turning toward righteousness. In the New Testament, "repent" is translated from a Greek word *metanoeo*, meaning "to change one's mind for better; heartily to amend with abhorrence for one's past sins."[7] When we repent from offense, we change our mind about accepting it and refuse to tolerate it.

As mentioned previously, offense contains five transgressions: Anger, Bitterness, Judgment, Unforgiveness, and Pride. As we've seen, every time you operate in offense, whether it is in your thoughts, words, or actions, you engage in five sins that will produce consequences in your life. The wonderful news is that when you repent from offense, you also turn away from all five transgressions that were involved in the offensive incident, and therefore cancel the subsequent consequences.

Repentance is beautiful and brings so many benefits. It realigns you with God's design and purpose and frees you from

---

7 *Strong's Concordance*

Repentance is beautiful and brings many benefits. It realigns you with God's design and purpose and frees you from the enemy's deception and plans.

---

the enemy's deception and plans. Repentance makes way for personal revival and refreshment as well as entrance into Kingdom life. Lack of repentance creates diminished quality of life. The following scriptures confirm this:

Acts 3:19

"Therefore repent and return, so that your sins may be wiped away, in order that times of refreshing may come from the presence of the Lord."

Matthew 4:17

"From that time Jesus began to preach and say, 'Repent, for the kingdom of heaven is at hand.'"

Luke 13:3

"I tell you, no, but unless you repent, you will all likewise perish." (NASB1995)

Repenting from offense is not a one-time action; rather, every time we find ourselves taking offense, we change our mind about it and turn in the opposite direction. I have discovered that the more I catch myself in offense and repent, the less offended I become. In the beginning, I was convicted numerous times a day over some of the most subtle offenses. Now, I sometimes go days without awareness of even one conviction of sin in this area.

3. FORGIVENESS, CLEANSING, AND REPLACEMENT

Repentance is powerful, but Jesus also gave us the blessing of forgiveness and cleansing from the offense of which we've repented. In 1 John 1:9, we discover that if we confess our sins, He is faithful and just to forgive us and cleanse us from all unrighteousness. When we humbly come before the Lord, confessing that we engaged in an offensive thought, word, or deed and ask Him to forgive and cleanse us, He will. You don't need to do any penance or any works to deserve it. It is a gift, and your slate is clean afterward. You are justified—just as if you never sinned!

When you are forgiven and cleansed from offense with its five transgressions, the enemy has no ability to use the offense as a "landing strip" for his purposes. Jesus said, "...the prince of this world is coming. He has no hold over me" (John 14:30 NIV).

If you have shared your offense with others, go to those you shared with and ask them to forgive you. This will encourage them to receive freedom and will potentially keep the offense from spreading.

After you turn away from offense and receive cleansing from the transgressions involved, you will want to be filled with the spirit opposite of offense. Ask the Lord to fill you with His Spirit of unoffendable love. "Be filled with the Spirit." Don't leave the place vacant where offense was harbored, but let the Spirit of God fill the void. It is a type of spiritual "replacement therapy." Repent, Cleanse, Replace—Repent, Cleanse, Replace—Repent, Cleanse, Replace.

4. EMBRACE THE CROSS

Jesus taught His disciples to take up their cross daily and follow Him (Luke 9:23). The cross represents death and execution. In Bible times, many criminals who were sentenced to death were crucified—hung on a cross to die.

Two thousand years ago, Jesus died on the cross for you and me. On the cross, the blameless, selfless, pure Son of God, forgave us of all our sins and then literally gave Himself as a living sacrifice by dying in our place.

On the cross, He released us from penalty and judgment and reconciled us to the Father. He declared, "Father, forgive them for they know not what they do" (Luke 23:34). He held no offense against us, and yet, even in the crowd that stood before Him, there were those who slandered Him, betrayed Him, denied Him, abandoned Him, and rejected Him. Nothing could make Him withhold love from us. He gave His all for those He could have been offended with and that includes you and me.

Galatians 2:20 says,

"I have been crucified with Christ; and it is no longer I who live, but Christ lives in me; and the *life* which I now live in the flesh I live by faith in the Son of God, who loved me and gave Himself up for me."

Offense is very selfish and full of entitlement, but we are called to be like Christ and embrace the cross, refusing to take offense. When you embrace the cross, you not only forgive those who sin against you, but you die to your right to be offended. The cross represents death, so imagine a dead man trying to take offense—it is impossible. A dead man cannot take offense or retaliate in any way. If you are offended, you are not dead yet!

When we were students at a Discipleship Training School (DTS) in Youth With A Mission (YWAM), we jokingly re-named the DTS program the "Die To Self" school. In the training, we were constantly reminded that we had no "rights" if we were living the crucified life. We had no right to be treated well or with honor and respect. We had no right to position, financial benefits, or preferred treatment. How can a dead man demand such things? It was drilled into us that unless we died to self, Christ couldn't manifest His life in and through us. We had to choose who would live: Him or me?

The new life we receive through the miracle of our salvation is Christ's life. "Unless a grain of wheat falls into the earth and dies, it remains alone; but if it dies, it bears much fruit" (John 12:24). When I die, He lives.

I received the revelation of the cross when I was living in a season of great self-condemnation. Without intention, I made a careless mistake that deeply hurt someone. I asked for forgiveness, but they were not able to grant it initially. I beat myself up with condemnation regularly for this mistake and was tormented by self-accusation and guilt. I was deeply offended with myself!

One day, I was crying out to God in agony and remorse as I remembered my failure. Amid my tears, He took me into a revelation of the cross. He showed me that a dead man has no further responsibility for sins committed when they were alive. They are dead. You cannot punish a dead man. You cannot put him in jail and have him learn a lesson through it. You cannot beat him up and have it affect him. He is dead!

I began to laugh and rejoice! What a wonderful blessing! I am dead to my old life with its trespasses and sins. When Christ died on the cross, I died with Him and so did my transgressions. They are paid in full. I am forgiven. I am crucified with Christ, nevertheless, I live!! Christ IS my life, and He is unoffendable—all my offense died with Him on the cross two thousand years ago!

If you are engaged in offense, you are not dead yet. Embrace the cross in the moment you identify offense and die to your perceived right to be offended. "Likewise you also, reckon yourselves to be dead indeed to sin, but alive to God in Christ Jesus our Lord" (Romans 6:11). Then clothe yourself in Christ's beautiful unoffendable nature. Anyone can be offended. Being offendable is part of what could be termed "the low life of the Adamic nature," but when you are free from offense, you are living the quality "high life" you've been granted in Christ.

5. TURN YOUR ANGER TOWARD THE SIN AND AWAY FROM THE PERSON

As taught previously, it is important that you direct your anger toward the transgression and not the transgressor. This is what your Heavenly Father has done for you. He sent Jesus to pardon you but has poured out His wrath on the transgression.

—☙—

Embrace the cross in the moment you identify offense and die to your perceived right to be offended.

—☙—

Years ago, my ministry was involved in a concentrated season of emotional healing and deliverance. Many who had been sexually abused came for ministry. Understandably, they were angry and greatly offended at their abuser, and several of them had carried that pain for many years. I understood that for each of them to be free, they would need to move the anger and offense off their abuser and onto the sin.

I gave many of them a homework exercise which helped tremendously. It involved them writing a letter to their abuser that they would never deliver to them. I encouraged them to share their heart by communicating all they would like to say if they had the freedom to address them face-to-face.

The next time we met, they brought the letter with them. Most often, the letters began with a polite, "Dear John" and an opening sentence. As the letter progressed, the words became fiery, and even their handwriting became bolder and larger, often with many exclamation marks. They were able to fully express their offense with its anger, bitterness, judgment, unforgiveness, and pride. As they read their letters to me, they would cry deeply as emotions surfaced, and a few could not finish reading.

When they were ready, I helped them to go through the letter, and one line at a time, choose to forgive their abuser for the transgressions involved. At this point, they did not always feel the genuineness of their forgiveness, but they chose it regardless of their feelings or lack of them. The next step was to choose to move their offense with its five elements off their abuser and onto the actual transgressions. This process brought healing, deliverance, and empowerment.

We must separate the sin from the sinner. Holy Spirit will help us do this. It is important to remember that we are not battling flesh and blood, but invisible spiritual enemies who are filled with offense themselves and desire us to partake of their demonic nature.

6. WHAT DOES LOVE LOOK LIKE?

When we face temptation to take offense, we must remember who we are and Whose we are. God is LOVE and we are filled with His nature. Love does not take offense. Love believes the best and will always see value in someone. Jesus has been mistreated by all humanity, but He continually believes the best for all of us and never ceases to value us. We can do the same.

God promises that He will work everything together for good to those who love Him and who are called according to His purpose (Romans 8:28). Love will always offer a solution, and that is how you can make offensive opportunities work together for something good. Ask yourself the following question when tempted to take offense: "What does love look like in this situation?"

It is vital that you know how loved you are! In the midst of your pain, God cares. He loves you deeply. He is with you and for you, but He also loves and is committed to the one you are offended with. He loves them and wants them to come through their stuff. He does not take sides, yet, He is one hundred percent for you. Let's examine the following scripture:

Joshua 5:13-15

And it came to pass, when Joshua was by Jericho, that he lifted his eyes and looked, and behold, a Man stood opposite him with His sword drawn in His hand. And Joshua went to Him and said to Him, "Are You for us or for our adversaries?"

So He said, "No, but as Commander of the army of the Lord I have now come."

And Joshua fell on his face to the earth and worshiped, and said to Him, "What does my Lord say to His servant?"

Then the Commander of the LORD's army said to Joshua, "Take your sandal off your foot, for the place where you stand is holy." And Joshua did so. (NKJV)

Joshua had enemies to fight, and when the Lord showed up in physical manifestation, Joshua asked if He was for him and his people or their enemies. The Lord explained that He was on neither side but had come to lead in the battle for righteousness.

When we are hurt, we want everyone on our side and we expect those who are with us to stand against the one who hurt us. But how can we reconcile this when we take into account that Jesus died on the cross for everyone, even His most aggressive enemies? He died for the individual(s) who harmed you and desires them to come to full repentance and wholeness, breaking the cycle of hurting people hurting others. He died for your enemies as well as your friends. He loves your enemies as He loves you. This revelation is indeed holy ground.

When you are tempted to take hold of an offense, remember that the Lord is on the side of righteousness and love and not on the side of your offense. Ask Him what His love looks like for the person or persons you are offended with. When He shows you, ask Him to fill you with His heart for them. This is

—◊—

Jesus died for your enemies as well as your friends.
He loves your enemies as He loves you.
This revelation is indeed holy ground.

—◊—

very high ground, and He would love to walk the journey with you.

When you are hurt and mistreated, ask yourself, "What does love look like? How can I love them well? How can I be like Jesus? What would Jesus do?"

Years ago, a pastor was speaking slanderous things against me and my ministry from his pulpit and in the local ministerial meetings I attended. He was opposed theologically to some of our beliefs and was offended that I was a woman in ministry and ministered the Holy Spirit's gifts and glory. His negative and dishonoring words spread into our community. The Lord told me not to be concerned but to love him and the other pastors in the group well. So, I did. When I attended the ministerial meetings, I brought donuts and coffee and served them. They didn't like me sharing so I didn't, but I silently interceded for them, choosing to love and lay down any potential offense.

I gave the offended pastor personal financial gifts, as well as gifts to his ministry, and honored him publicly. I fought his cruelty with intentional and sincere love. Every time I heard of something he spoke against me, I forgave him and blessed him. I prayed for him and decreed God's goodness over him and his ministry. He began to tolerate me somewhat but never repented from his offense against me. My commitment to love him wasn't based on him eventually accepting me, it was a commitment I made to the Lord in order to fellowship with Christ's love sufferings.

Within a year, a tragedy took place. He was terminated as pastor of his church. It unfortunately became the talk of the town. When I heard it, I was grieved (not elated). I felt compassion for him and prayed for God to restore him. It was sad. Offense, with its five elements of anger, bitterness, judgment, unforgiveness and pride, impacted him—he bore the consequences. I continued to care about him and our ministry continued to flourish. The Lord blessed us year after year. When you resist offense and choose love, it brings great reward.

In an earlier chapter, I shared the story of our journey in the ministry of anti-trafficking. That whole aspect of our ministry was born out of a love response to the temptation of offense.

My friend, Heidi Baker, is an authentic apostle of love who lives in Mozambique, Africa, and ministers to the afflicted in nations around the world. She is a true missionary whom I admire. She has lived through horrific and tragic situations where words fail to describe the horror and terror of the circumstances. I have watched her time after time choose love over offense. She never quit loving when terrorists murdered those she loved. She continued to pray for them and reach out to them with the gospel and with acts of love. She hated the injustices but used her anger to rescue and love many into the Kingdom. Love changes everything!

7. PRAYER

We have been given the privilege of approaching God in prayer and making our requests known, but too often we fail to activate the blessing. James says, "You have not because you ask not…"(James 4:2b). According to 1 John 5:14-15, when we pray according to God's will, He grants us our request. Ask the Lord to give you an unoffendable heart. It seems very elementary and simple, but so often we complicate our walk with the Lord. You are not on your own in this battle against offense. The Lord loves to enable and empower you to fulfill your desire. Have you asked for His help?

Jesus gave us a key in Mark 11:24, "Therefore, I say to you, all things for which you pray and ask, believe that you have received them, and they will be granted to you." The key is that you need to receive the answer before it manifests. When do you receive an unoffendable heart? WHEN you pray. By faith receive your unoffendable heart. From the moment you pray, your request is received in heaven and granted. It might take time for it to fully manifest, but it is yours from that moment if you receive it.

Daniel fasted and prayed for three weeks without seeing any breakthrough, but when the angel came with a message, he said, "… from the first day that you set your heart on under-standing this and on humbling yourself before your God, your words were heard, and I have come in response to your words" (Daniel 10:12).

Have confidence that when you ask God for an unoffendable heart, He is on it and will partner with you in the journey.

I personally love praying in tongues to strengthen my goal. In 1 Corinthians 14:4, we are taught that when we pray in tongues, we edify ourselves (build ourselves up). I want to be edified with an unoffendable heart. I believe for this when I pray in tongues.

8. PRAISE AND THANKSGIVING

Praise is powerful and can shift mindsets within you. If you find yourself tempted to take offense, begin to praise the Lord and thank Him for His blessings. It could sound something like this: "Lord, I praise You and thank You for the pure heart You have created in me that is full of love. You have given me a heart just like Yours—a beautiful, unoffendable heart! I praise You, Lord, that You are guarding my heart and keeping me from stumbling into offense. You are my light and my salvation, and I exalt You as ruler and king of my heart and life."

9. COMMUNION

I have found communion to be a powerful discipline in the Lord. When we partake of the elements representing Christ's body and blood, we remember Him. By faith, I like to partake of His unoffendable nature when I receive communion. You can take communion at home on your own with the Lord. You do not have to be in a church service or have a minister serve it to you, and you can partake of communion as often as you desire. In 1 Corinthians 11, we are encouraged to examine ourselves before we partake. The teaching on communion in 1 Corinthians 11 is in the context of betrayal and divisions in the church. Issues of betrayal and division are rooted in offense, so it is important that we search our hearts before we partake. When we fail to do so, and if we harbor offense in our heart, Paul calls this taking communion in an unworthy manner, and as a result of this, many are weak, sick, and dying.

When taking communion, ask the Holy Spirit to convict you of any area of offense, and repent before you eat and drink of the elements. Then partake of the elements, remembering Jesus – Unoffendable Jesus. Partake of His nature. Be filled with His love.

10. REMEMBER WHO YOU ARE

You are a child of God, created in the image and likeness of God. Like Jesus, you are without offense in your spirit. You are a new creation in Christ, old things have passed away and all things have become new (2 Corinthians 5:17). Do not identify with an evil nature, filled with anger, bitterness, judgment, unforgiveness, and pride. That is NOT who you are. You are loving, kind, merciful, precious, and unoffendable!

I like making decrees of who I am in Christ as a reminder of who Christ has made me to be. I highly recommend, proclaiming the truth of your new nature over your life daily. It will help you to be reminded. James reveals a confirming truth:

Do not identify with an evil nature, filled with anger, bitterness, judgment, unforgiveness and pride. That is NOT who you are. You are loving, kind, merciful, precious, and unoffendable.

James 1:23-24

"For if anyone is a hearer of the word and not a doer, he is like a man who looks at his natural face in a mirror; for once he has looked at himself and gone away, he has immediately forgotten what kind of person he was."

Don't forget who you are!

WHEN YOU ARE THE ONE SOMEONE IS OFFENDED WITH

Proverbs 18:19 says,

"A brother offended is harder to win than a strong city, And contentions are like the bars of a castle." (NASB1995)

No one wakes up in the morning purposely desiring to offend someone, but as we've seen, offenses do happen. Sometimes we give opportunity to offend because we have been careless with our words or actions, and sometimes we give opportunity to offend because of no words and no actions.

Years ago, I received a phone call late one night from a woman who identified herself by name. I did not recognize the name and asked how I knew her. She proceeded to tell me that I was the reason she had suffered mental illness and breakdown for ten years. Of course, I was shocked and asked for more details. She explained that I had spoken at a conference many years previously. After my session, she came to greet me, but apparently, I walked right past her, ignoring her. She told me the rejection was too much to bear, and it started a cycle of breakdowns that resulted in hospitalizations for long periods. Her therapist encouraged her to call me.

I was without words at first and then tried to comfort her with the fact that I would never intentionally desire to reject her. I suggested that perhaps I was on my way to the bathroom during the short break between sessions, and my focus on getting to the restroom limited my scope of attention. I wasn't sharing this to defend myself but in hopes she would be brought to peace. I apologized the best I could and offered to pray for her.

Matthew 5:23-26 teaches us that if we know someone has something against us, we are to settle it quickly.

"Therefore, if you are offering your gift at the altar and there remember that your brother or sister has something against you, leave your gift there in front of the altar. First go and be reconciled to them; then come and offer your gift.

"Settle matters quickly with your adversary who is taking you to court. Do it while you are still together on the way, or your adversary may hand you over to the judge, and the judge may hand you over to the officer, and you may be thrown into prison. Truly I tell you, you will not get out until you have paid the last penny." (NIV)

If we have done wrong, we need to make it right and ask them to forgive us. Humility is the best posture. If you have made things right, asked for forgiveness and they've refused, choosing instead to hold on to their offense, bring them before the Lord and ask Him to help them.

Forgive them for their unforgiveness and offense toward you and pray for them. Don't be defensive in thoughts, words, or deeds, and do not take an offense against them for their unforgiveness toward you. Forgive yourself and ask God to forgive you of the transgression, and then give them to God. He knows the best way to help them, and He knows you have done your best to make things right. You can move on, leaving everything in God's hands.

THE BLESSINGS OF OVERCOMING OFFENSE

When you resist offense (with its five elements of anger, bitterness, judgment, unforgiveness and pride), and choose love, miracles happen. We have seen many "turn arounds" in lives as they chose to repent from offense.

Healing

My ministry friend, Katie Souza, has understood the devastating consequences of offense for many years. As a result, in her public meetings, she ministers healing and deliverance following times of repentance from offense. She has seen hundreds of miracles because of this specific focus. Diseases such as cancer, arthritis, heart issues, migraines, autoimmune disorders, and many other conditions disappear following freedom from offense.

We have also seen numerous healings from a variety of mental illnesses and emotional tensions like anxiety, tormenting fears, and night terrors. When offense is fully dealt with, the body, soul, and spirit come into healing.

Restored Relationships

Offense damages relationships, but when the offense is dealt with, healing and reconciliation follow. When you are offended, you see the person through the lens of that offense—their faults, flaws, and failures are magnified. But when you turn from offense, you will see the beautiful things God has invested in them—their attributes are magnified and their faults, flaws, and failures are diminished in your sight. Marriages are restored, friendships are renewed, and relationships in the workplace, church, and family are brought into health and healing.

Renewed Testimony

Offense damages your testimony, but when you replace your offense with love, patience, and kindness, people are attracted to your Christ-like nature and will be open to receiving from you.

While living and ministering in the inner city of Honolulu, amongst drug addicts, prostitutes, pimps, murderers, and lawless individuals, we chose to be purposely unoffendable in order to represent Christ. One day while sharing with a downtrodden prostitute in the courtyard, she responded with thanksgiving saying, "We all watch you and have been waiting for you to show your disgust in us, but you just keep loving and accepting."

We had been living in this inner city for a couple of months with no visible fruit. We didn't realize that we were being evaluated by those who lived there. They had experienced cruelty, judgment, and offense from Christians in the past and thought it was just a matter of time before our team showed our true colors. Soon after that, we reaped a harvest and many came to know Jesus with authentic faith and trust.

Offense destroys your testimony. Build your testimony with unoffendable love.

Financial Breakthrough

I know individuals who held offense toward those who believed in the doctrine of prosperity. They argued the doctrine from a position of offense rather than engaging in a healthy debate to discover truth. As a result, they spread their offense to others, and, unfortunately, many were experiencing lack in their personal lives as a result. During a particular ministry time in a conference, I invited those who related to being offended in this way to repent, receive forgiveness, and open their hearts to receive from the Lord. The altar was full. Numbers of testimonies were shared over time regarding the breakthroughs they received in their personal financial situations as a result. Offense had held back their blessings, but repentance had produced their freedom.

Spiritual Growth and Revival

Offense blocks your spiritual growth and hinders your relationship with the Lord. Sin separates us from God, and our prayers are hindered from being answered. When we repent from offense, our spiritual life becomes vibrant and full. One time I was in prayer repenting before the Lord from an offense I had taken. As I was still praying, a flood of the Lord's presence washed over me. I could feel His delight. I had been feeling spiritually dull prior to that, and suddenly everything changed. I was experiencing spiritual revival in the very presence of the Lord immediately following my repentance.

As mentioned in an earlier chapter, Revelation 12:10 declares that when accusation is cast down, then salvation, power, the Kingdom of God and the authority of Christ manifest. It begins with you and me!

DREAM BIG WITH ME!

It gives me great delight to share this book with you—my journey of learning to live unoffendable. I pray it will become your journey too.

As we complete the book, I want to invite you to dream. Dream about yourself being free from all offense and baptized in love, righteousness, and wisdom. Dream about your family being filled with the glory of unoffendable love. Dream about your city, region, and nation being filled with people who refuse to take offense and who choose only love. Dream about those in your workplace, schools, hospitals, and marketplaces overflowing with sweet love, everyone preferring each other. Dream about the church being a beautiful community and family who love each other and those in the world they live in well—a family of believers refusing offense.

I love these dreams because they are God's dreams. When they come to pass one day, then the prayer Jesus taught us to pray is fulfilled: "Your Kingdom come, Your will be done on earth as it is in heaven." You can be part of bringing God's dream to pass. It is what Jesus died for. It is what Jesus lives for!

I invite you to dream.
Dream about yourself being free from all offense and
baptized in love, righteousness, and wisdom.

Bonus Message

"Jesus Gazing"

To watch the message, place your phone camera over the
QR code and click on the link that appears.

EPILOGUE

"Therefore let us go on and get past the elementary stage in the teachings and doctrine of Christ (the Messiah), advancing steadily toward the completeness and perfection that belong to spiritual maturity."

—*Hebrews 6:1 (AMPC)*

THE EPILOGUE IS A "MUST-READ!"

Evangelist Katie Souza for decades lived a life of lawlessness and was incarcerated in a federal prison for crimes committed. She encountered the Lord during her prison sentence and was transformed by His love and truth. As one who was "all in" from the very moment Christ reached her, she influenced many prisoners around her to also come to Christ. Since that time, she has ministered in many prisons around the nation, has authored many resources, produced and hosted television programs, and preached the gospel on countless platforms.

She has a big heart, full of love and genuine care for those who suffer with oppression, and has given her life to seeing captives set free and healed. She loves well, is committed to righteousness, and is empowered by the Holy Spirit to work miracles.

Her epilogue is an important call and message. It might sound a little "rough and tough," but the black and white presentation represents her personality... and sometimes it's just what we need. I can assure you that her heart is filled with passionate love and fervent hope and faith for those who read this timely exhortation.

Patricia King

EPILOGUE

by Katie Souza

SNAP OUT OF IT

Let me make a confession to you at the beginning of this epilogue: I needed this book! We all have areas that we need to overcome in the area of offense, but my battle is to be unoffended at the church when I see believers filled with offense!

According to Psalm 8, all believers have been given dominion over all the works of God's hands. Yet, we are still sick, broken, and powerless when it comes to affecting real change in our own lives and in this earth. Why is that? It is my conviction that in many cases, the culprit is offense! Offense is the bitter root that troubles and defiles many. Still, we often fail to stop embracing this life-sucking behavior even though we know better.

Offense demonstrates the immature state of the church, and is blocking our entrance into the advanced things of the Spirit, those deep things of God that lead to massive breakthrough. Look at this eye-opening passage in Hebrews 6:1-3 (AMPC).

> Therefore let us go on and get past the elementary stage in the teachings and doctrine of Christ (the Messiah), advancing steadily toward the completeness and perfection

that belong to spiritual maturity. Let us not again be laying the foundation of repentance and abandonment of dead works (dead formalism) and of the faith [by which you turned] to God, With teachings about purifying, the laying on of hands, the resurrection from the dead, and eternal judgment and punishment. [These are all matters of which you should have been fully aware long, long ago.] If indeed God permits, we will [now] proceed [to advanced teaching].

Notice how repentance is cited here as an elementary teaching and doctrine of Christ. Regardless, the church is constantly needing to be reminded and even persuaded to repent of offense! I have taught soul healing for over a decade. During that time, I have administrated countless physical miracles with a large percentage manifesting after someone repented for being offended. I've seen metal dissolve, tumors shrink, pain leave the body, and every assorted disease eradicated. Shaking off the anger, unforgiveness, and bitterness found in offense ushers in incredible miracles! But still, many are constantly having to be reminded to repent as they hold on to their offense as if their lives depended on it. This is sad indeed.

Hebrews 6 drills in a very important truth. *Let us not again be laying the foundation of repentance and abandonment of dead works.* Holding on to bitterness and unforgiveness are dead works that instill no life whatsoever! Rather, they exhibit the childish behaviors that have the body of Christ "stuck like chuck." Hebrews 6 is very clear. These elementary matters *are all things of which we should have been fully aware long, long ago!*

Countless times, I've been stopped by someone after a meeting asking me if I can pray for them. This often happens when it's very late and the doors are already being shut. I always stop to help them out; many times, Holy Spirit will give me a name of someone with whom they are offended. After they confirm it's true, I often ask why they didn't forgive them in the meeting, during the many times that I led people through repentance and forgiveness. They never have a reasonable response, and I am left warring in the middle of the night for their healing. Situations like this give me opportunity to resist my own temptation to be offended with those who won't deal with their offense.

If I were to bottom-line the issue, I'd say, "Let's snap out of it!" People wonder why they never get healed or experience breakthrough. Holding on to offense is one of the key reasons! We've got a planet to rule and reign. Let's take off those diapers, pull that baby bottle out of our mouths, and move on to the advanced teachings of God! Every time an opportunity comes to get offended, resist it. Then ask the Holy Spirit to heal the wound that came from that conflict, instead of holding on to the reaction of offense.

Do as the Apostle Paul instructed in 1 Corinthians 11:31 (AMPC): *For if we searchingly examined ourselves [detecting our shortcomings and recognizing our own condition], we should not be judged and penalty decreed [by the divine judgment].* We should be laboring to forgive and forget by asking God to judge that wickedness in our own souls instead of judging others.

It's not surprising to find the above verse in the chapter where Paul teaches on the proper way to partake of communion. He opens with this:

For in the first place, when you assemble as a congregation, I hear that there are cliques (divisions and factions) among you; and I in part believe it, For doubtless there have to be factions or parties among you in order that they who are genuine and of approved fitness may become evident and plainly recognized among you.

Paul diagnosed that there was rampant offense in the body that manifested in divisions and factions. We still deal with these issues today. Notice that he stated these opportunities to become offended would show forth those who are genuine and approved by God. I want to be genuine and approved by God—how about you?

With all these divisions and factions in the church, no wonder there is so much sickness and death in the church. A warning Paul expressed in his next pen stroke:

> Examine your motives, test your heart, come to this meal in holy awe. If you give no thought (or worse, don't care) about the broken body of the Master when you eat and drink, you're running the risk of serious consequences. That's why so many of you even now are listless and sick, and others have gone to an early grave... For if we searchingly examined ourselves [detecting our shortcomings and recognizing our own condition], we should not be judged and penalty decreed [by the divine judgment]. (vv. 28-30 MSG/ v. 31 AMPC)

As this study ends, I highly suggest you go into deep worship. Prostrate yourself humbly before the Lord, and LET GO OF ALL OFFENSE in every form. Partake of His supper and then move forward to *get past the elementary stage in the teachings and doctrine of Christ (the Messiah), advancing steadily toward the completeness and perfection that belong to spiritual maturity.*

You have just completed a valuable and potentially life-transforming book. Don't let your reading be fruitless, but for the rest of your life on this earth, guard your heart so that you can master all future attempts of the devil to retake the ground that he has lost.

Be blessed,

Katie

About Patricia King

Patricia King is a respected apostolic and prophetic minister of the gospel. She is an accomplished itinerant speaker, author, television host, media producer, and ministry network overseer who has given her life fully to Jesus Christ and to His Kingdom's advancement in the earth.

She is the founder of Patricia King Ministries, Women in Ministry Network and Everlasting Love Academy. She has written many books and has produced an abundance of resources on digital media. She is also a successful business owner and an inventive entrepreneur. Patricia's reputation in the Christian community is world-renowned.

To Connect:

Patricia King website: PatriciaKing.com

Women in Ministry Network: WIMNglobal.com

Facebook: Facebook.com/PatriciaKingPage

Instagram: PatriciaKingPage

YouTube: https://www.youtube.com/c/PatriciaKingPage

Patricia King Academy: EverlastingLoveAcademy.com

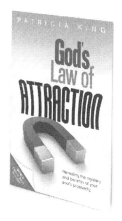

EXPOSED
WITCHCRAFT IN THE CHURCH

Witchcraft in the church? Yes. It is operating in the church today and many are suffering under its blatant and brutal assaults because there is lack of awareness.

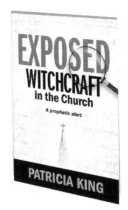

We must no longer deny its existence or live in fear. Above all, we must not passively shrug it off and do nothing about it. Rather, it is time to expose it for what it is and begin to use the powerful spiritual weapons that we have in Christ to defeat it.

NARCISSISM EXPOSED

Patricia King delves into the psychological and spiritual roots of narcissism, a disorder that is running rampant in both the world and the church. As you read, you will learn what narcissism is and how it manifests, how it takes root in an individual, the truth about narcissism in the church today, how to live with someone who is under of influence of a spirit of narcissism, and much more. A must read!

UNLOCK YOUR LIFE'S FULL POTENTIAL

Create Your World will empower you to frame your world and experience the kind of life Jesus died to give you. Extraordinary truths are presented with clear and simple guidelines to live a life of victory rather than a life of defeat. As you read and apply the principles, your relationships, health, finances, and overall state of being will be supernaturally blessed by God!

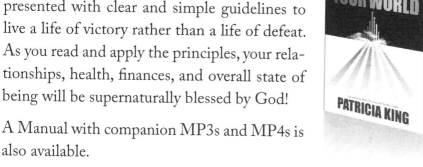

A Manual with companion MP3s and MP4s is also available.

YOU HAVE SUPERNATURAL SENSES

Just as He gave us five natural senses, God also created us with five spiritual senses. Cultivate your spiritual senses and learn how to see, hear, feel, taste, and smell more of the supernatural realm that is all around you.

This book is is a doorway to encounters that will answer the cry of your heart to know Him and His Kingdom more fully and intimately.

A USB which includes eBook, eStudy-Manual, MP3 Teachings and Audiobook is also available.

MORE BOOKS AND RESOURCES
BY PATRICIA KING

Available at PatriciaKing.com

RECEIVE A GLORIOUS REVELATION

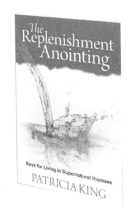

Discover a path of miracle replenishment and increase in everything that pertains to you – your physical strength, your love, your time, your provision, your gifts, your anointing, and anything else that flows from you to God and others.

Receive this God-given revelation through biblical examples, insights and keys, along with practical applications, personal testimonies, and decrees for activation.

EXPERIENCE FINANCIAL BREAKTHROUGH

You were created to know abundance and blessing. Not only is God well able to prosper His people, but He has given us the tools to lay hold of abundance right now. Patricia opens your eyes to God's prosperity plan for you and gives you powerful Scripture-based decrees to open heaven's windows of blessing over your life.

The Word of God never returns void; it always produces fruit. Grab hold of these decrees and get your financial breakthrough!

Additional copies of this book and other
book titles from Patricia King are available at:

Patriciaking.com
Amazon.com

Bulk/wholesale prices for stores and ministries:

Please contact: resource@PatriciaKing.com

Made in the USA
Columbia, SC
14 December 2022

73926717R00080